THE STORY OF ANTRIM

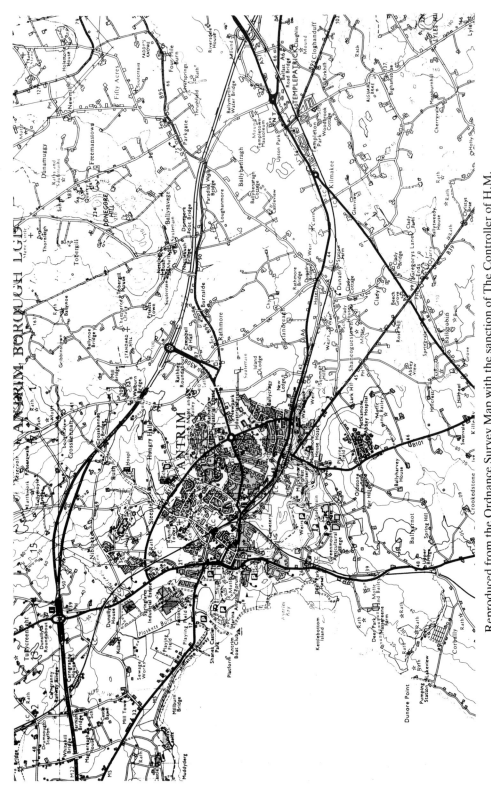

Reproduced from the Ordnance Survey Map with the sanction of The Controller of H.M.
Stationery Office, Crown Copyright Reserved.

Alastair Smyth is Chairman of Antrim & District Historical Society, Head of the English Department at Antrim Grammar School and an experienced writer of drama, documentaries, short stories and talks commissioned by the BBC, RTE and Ulster Television. He moved to Mid-Antrim in 1950 and lives with his wife and two daughters in Antrim town.

THE STORY
OF ANTRIM

The story of the great and the near great, the wise and otherwise, the rich and the poor of Ulster's historic county town of Antrim – from the prehistoric past to modern times.

by

ALASTAIR SMYTH

First Edition
A (1984) NATIONAL HERITAGE YEAR PUBLICATION

Published 1984 by
ANTRIM BOROUGH COUNCIL, Antrim

Printed and Bound by Nicholson and Bass Ltd

for
Zoë *and* Karen

ACKNOWLEDGEMENTS

To The Rt Hon. Lords Massereene (Chilham Castle) and O'Neill (Shane's Castle), in particular, I express my thanks both for their encouragements and kind permissions to use copyright materials.

For other copyright permissions I am indebted to O.S. (N.I.) Chief Survey Officer, the Deputy Keeper of Public Records for Northern Ireland (PRONI), *Sunday News,* Northern Ireland Tourist Board, Controller of Her Majesty's Stationery Office, the Ulster Museum, Randalstown photographer – Pat McGuigan, and Antrim artists – Bob Ross and Rodney Gillen.

Grateful acknowledgement is also due to Antrim Borough Council and, in particular, Mr S. Magee, Clerk of Council, and Mr R. Woods, Principal Administrative Officer, for all their encouragements, helpful support and sponsorship.

For help of various kinds in my researches, particular thanks are due to Mrs Anna Irvine Buck, the Misses Dorothy Clarke, Violet Lynn, and Madeline and Margaret Smith, Dr R. M. Buchanan (Queen's University), Mr John Bell, B.Sc., Cllr. Robert Burns, Mr Ferguson Grainger, Dr D. B. McNeill (Ulster Museum), Messrs Patrick Coyle, Vincent Phelim and Louis Reford. And I am deeply indebted to the late Messrs. George Fleming and James Creighton – both greatly respected gentlemen on the late Lord Massereene's Staff – for their most friendly and informative assistance in the preparation of this book.

To these, and to all who have helped in any way – especially my dear wife, Irene, who has been such a cheerfully patient and efficient secretary – I express my most sincere thanks.

Alastair Smyth, *Antrim*

THE STORY OF ANTRIM

Contents

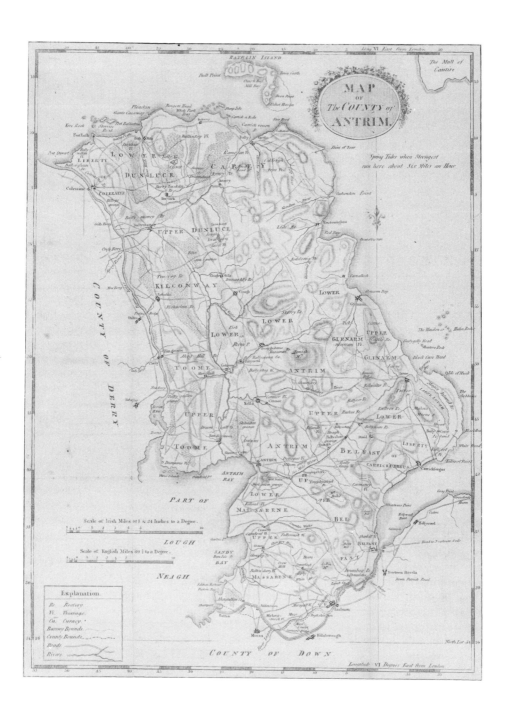

Author's Preface

'The Story of Antrim' presents us with two action-packed books in one: the variety of tales of happiness and woe, of saints and scholars, lords, ladies and vagabonds of Old Antrim mirrors much of the story of Ulster itself. I hope it is more than just a good story, however, packed though it is with ancient and mysterious pagan clansmen, fierce Viking raiders, mail-clad Norman knights and swashbuckling Elizabethan adventurers, or such tragic love stories as that of the young Antrim girl who might have become Queen of the United Kingdom. I hope that it will also serve as a companion to enrich the reader's travels around this most historically important and interesting district.

'Remember the days of old,' the Scriptures enjoin us; 'consider the years of many generations: ask thy father, and he will shew thee; thy elders, and they will tell thee,' (Deut. 32, v. 7). And Cicero advised: 'To be ignorant of what happened before you were born is to remain forever a child.' My distinguished Antrim forefather and local historian, W. S. Smith, agreed: 'A knowledge of the past enables us to appreciate the present, to realise more vividly than we otherwise could, the fact that the present is the outgrowth, the product, the message of the past.' Our own behaviour, for example, is often governed by ancient customs, particularly at life's main turning points: such things as what one should or should not do at weddings, christenings, funerals, house-warmings or when visiting a new-born baby for the first time. We, in Ulster, remain the last Europeans to light Hallowe'en bonfires and so perpetuate the 2,000 years old Gaelic New Year's Eve celebration. 'Orange' bonfires are the outgrowth of the old Beltaine fires lit by our ancestors on May 1 (from the Gaelic name for May, 'Bealtaine'), to drive away witches and evil spirits. Our popular Mothering Sunday (celebrated on mid-Lent Sunday), dates from pre-Reformation times when parishioners returned to the Mother Church to offer gifts. St Valentine's Day stems from a pagan fertility festival. As W. S. Smith concluded: 'To know something of the past is to be prepared to understand the present.'

To see the truth whole, however, is neither possible nor is it my intention; there can be no such thing as a final analysis in recording local history. In attempting an Olympian survey of the complex web of Antrim's social, political, religious, economic, cultural (etc.) past, sins of omission are inevitable and, often, unfortunately deliberate. Nevertheless, I trust that my readers will enjoy (and benefit from) being wafted across the centuries. Those who wish to pursue any thematic element may find useful the select bibliography provided at the end of the book.

Perhaps this publication, in affording some glimpses of an intriguing past, will serve as a quarry of a book to stimulate others to enquire further; to quote Qoheleth, 'of making many books there is no end' (Eccles. 12, v. 12). And, there is a need for us, who are creatures of but a day in the story of Antrim, to collect, conserve, interpret and securely display locally those objects which best serve to illustrate the history of Antrim.

Antrim 1980 – Courtesy of *Sunday News*.

THE STORY OF ANTRIM

IN THE BEGINNING

Out of fire, ice and water the district of Antrim was formed.

Antrim's story begins 'in the beginning' with the big bang when the earth was born. There's not much we can see today of those times but we can reach back nearly 300 million years.

Our little corner of the globe was once part of a vast, torrid desert. After a mere 30 million years of sunshine, however, great tidal waves rolled in to submerge the sands. County Antrim was born when the waters broke some 50 million years later.

Just as chalk-Antrim rose dramatically from the seabed, it was thrown into the melting pot for another 20 million years. A 'subterranean thunder rumbled beneath the sandstones and limestones of Antrim. Terrific vents cracked open in its surface and molten lava from the earth's core streamed out, flaming and hissing. Ten thousand Vulcans, blowing their bellows in their subterranean workshops for the production of volcanoes, would have been no more than pygmies in comparison with the work done'.[28] At the time, N. America was literally the next parish west of Ulster and this parting of their ways was objected to by volcanic outbursts from Skye through Antrim to Lundy Island.

When the lava solidified, weathering encouraged the growth of plants and animal life. Then further eruptions sent basaltic lava flowing from the great fissure of Dunluce in the north to Scrabo in the south. But towering above the massy basaltic plateau stood the great rock of Tardree. The beautiful and highly distinctive 'Tardree rhyolite' – another igneous rock but much earlier than the more familiar black basalt of Antrim – is very rarely found in these islands. In the 19th century it brought a unique dressing to many of Antrim's important buildings.

In local quarries (and along our east coast), we find excellent cross-sections of the hard, black volcanic basalt overlying the original sedimentary chalk. Running through the middle of the basalts is a band of reddish rock – graphically visible at Ladyhill quarry – which marks where the first great series of lava-flows ceased, cooled and hardened. The primitive forms of animal life and vegetation (supported by the soil created by weathering), were petrified into this reddish inter-basaltic bed upon the second (upper layer of basalt) series of volcanic activity.

Black basalt-built buildings are familiar to us all. This rock has long provided men of Antrim with a cheap building material in abundant supply. But for Antrim men – indeed, man himself – there is still no place in our story.

At the close of that fiery Miocene Age, much of County Antrim was covered by a great lough. Then all was obliterated with an Arctic landscape for thousands of years more, the land locked in the grip of a succession of ice ages. Sheets of ice, up to six thousand feet thick, travelled south over the country, grinding down the basaltic hills and mountains. When they beat their final retreat, about eighteen thousand years ago, they carved out the great Glens of Antrim. And the sea returned to fashion the land ready for man; beds of gravels, sand and small boulders were deposited.

Antrim's 19th century distinguished citizen, Rev. W. S. Smith observed: 'In the exposed embankment, between the bridge over the Belfast Road and Moylena crossing of the Northern Counties Railway, we find great variety in the arrangement of the loose, drift material, produced during submergence; the level sand-bed, the little mound, and the heap of small boulders. Near Antrim, in various directions, there are rounded, gracefully-sloping mounds of hillocks, most of which, if cut in twain, would reveal a structure similar to the railway embankment.' As late as the last century, local people referred to the land between Church Street and the Massereene Hospital as 'the Strand'.

1

Finally, after the last glaciers disappeared but before our morainic land-bridge with Britain was submerged, some plants, trees and animals (like the Great Elk) arrived to complete their pilgrimage from north-western Europe. The principal trees were willow, birch, hazel, pine, alder, oak, elm and ash. Many species were too late to make the crossing: the beech and the lime, among trees; of animals – toads, moles, weasels and, of course, snakes; and the woodpecker and nut-hatch among birds.

The stage was now set for man. Valuable flints in the chalk cliffs of Antrim's coast glittered to attract man across the narrow North Channel. The year was somewhere around 7000 B.C.

ANTRIM ABORIGINES

The first Antrim men were also the first Irish men and they hailed from mainland Britain (or, more precisely, Scotland; or more precisely still, Pictland, as Scotland was then).

These prehistoric 'Brits' made their way to Lough Neagh's northern shores, in skin-covered curraghs, by pursuing eels up the Lower Bann. Mesolithic fishers and hunters were not attracted into our huge tracts of primeval forest; the province of bison herds, giant deer, bears and packs of wolves.

Middle East farmers began arriving around 3500 B.C. They sowed wheat to make bread, kept cattle, sheep, pigs, asses, cats and dogs, and began weaving cloth and spinning flax into linen.

Antrim's earliest prehistoric monuments date from the New Stone Age; 4000–2000 B.C. To clear parts of the extensive forests for farming, Stone Age men used stone axes; finely polished axe-heads and arrow heads may still be found locally. At Lyles Hill (2 miles south-east of Templepatrick), these Neolithic businessmen operated an important pottery-manufacturing industry. Enormous quantities of decorated pottery, stone axes and flint implements have been uncovered there. In 1953, excavations at Langford Lodge (at the loughshore south of Antrim), uncovered a Neolithic site of possible ceremonial or religious significance.

A most impressive megalithic passage-grave stands in a field beside the old Roughfort rath, 2½ miles from Templepatrick: nine covered chambers successively rise in height over a distance of 45 ft. to form 'Carn Grainne'; one of the 'beds' where legend says Princess Grainne slept when Celtic warriors pursued her across Ireland. (Grainne fled from Tara when her royal father arranged for her to marry the aged Finn MacCuil, or MacCool!)

Carn Grainne was surrounded by a circle of standing stones until the 18th century. The forty-one stones arranged in a circle at Kilmakee, Dunadry (the J209852 'Cairn' of the 1981 O.S. map), were either a druidical ceremonial centre or made for a calendrical purpose. Stone circles (which were not burial places), have also been located locally at Tobergill and Moyadam, near Parkgate.

At Drumagorgan there was once a 'rocking stone' glacial erratic (under which 16th century criminals and innocents were literally rocked to death). A warrior of unusually large stature, according to an ancient tale, made his last stand in battle in the townland of Drumagorgan. (Tradition holds that a wide ditch – running straight from the Holestone to Shane's Castle area – formed an ancient boundary between the dominions of the above warrior and another Irish chieftain.) The hill where he raised his standard is still known as Standard Hill. His 'Giant's Grave' is the 'Chambered Grave' (J191887) of the 1981 O.S. map. Antrim man, John Boal, decided to test the truth of that tradition during the early years of the 19th century. Inside the grave he found an extraordinarily large skeleton with the remnants of a fiercesome sword and shield (which he delivered to the museum in Belfast).

Old Stone, at Muckamore, takes its name from an 8 ft tall by 4 ft thick standing stone which stood at that hill until the last century when it was senselessly toppled into the Sixmilewater. Ten massive grey whinstones anciently marked the local end of the 13 ft broad 'Irish Highway' (Slighe Miodhluchra) connecting the sea at Carrickfergus with the ford at Toome (via Antrim). The tenth stone – 'the Gray Stone' – gave its name to the hill above Antrim – 'the Gray-Stone Brae' (now the Greystone Road).

A second ancient, paved road (for crossing the bogs) which has been excavated locally is the 9 ft wide 'Priest Causeway'. The 18½-miles-long Sixmilewater river could be forded at Muckamore and the ancients paved the riverbed there with large, flat stones. It was an important crossing on the route from Tara to Dunseverick.

Part of the Druids' Altar, Browndod.

The most-haunting monuments of Antrim's prehistoric past must be those megaliths which make Browndod Hill, Antrim's Stonehenge. The present writer couldn't resist the easy climb after noting the following passage in Donegore's 1833–38 O.S. Memoir:

> "The remains on this hill consist of two comparatively perfect altars and one imperfect one; four tumuli; fifteen enclosures of various forms; the foundations of two buildings; a standing stone; and several ancient roads and paths."

For the untrained eye (with some difficulty, admittedly), there is much to discover (short distances to the north and north-west of the triangulation station) on high Browndod. But unmistakably, in the field just a few yards immediately north of the summit, stands the truly and spectactulary dramatic 'Druidical Altar' megalith, (excavated 1934). Despite popular belief, there exists no evidence of druidical practices or presence here. (There is a lone Fairy Thorn tree, however!) The Western Neolithic prehistoric peoples who built this long and horned, collective-burial chamber tomb may have originated in Britain or Atlantic France. The Altar is 40 feet long and divided into four burial chambers (each chamber measuring 8 feet by 3½ feet), and all opening off a wedge-shaped forecourt.

Beside the cairn on Donegore Hill, preliminary excavations (1984) of what is probably the finest, extensive Neolithic settlement site in the British Isles – unique in Ireland – are yielding artefacts in abundance and our first hard evidence of the way of life in Ireland 5,000 years ago. Though there was extensive Neolithic occupation of Lyles Hill, its 13 acre hilltop fort is probably of Late Bronze or Iron Age date.

One Bronze Age standing stone which is worth visiting stands near the Holestone Crossroads (just beyond the Owens family's Holestone House in the former 18th

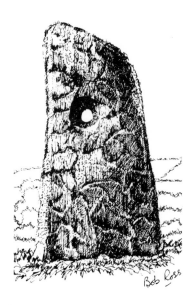

century deerpark of the Marquis of Donegall). The 5 feet high Holestone megalith is curiously pierced with a countersunk four-inch-diameter hole. Was this made for some magical rite in this obvious Eldorado vicinity of pagan times? Perhaps its reputation for admitting (only female) hands and its use by troth-plighting couples in the last century, stems from an ancient practice of solemnising marriages or concluding solemn treaties by the joining of hands? Whatever the purpose, the Holestone remains the finest Bronze Age whinstone pillar of its type in the British Isles; and very fortunate it was that the farmer who once removed most of the surrounding rockbase agreed to leave this curiosity for posterity. Outstanding in its own field, you might say!

The Holestone.

THE CELTS

From about five centuries before the time of Christ, barbaric groups of Celtic-speaking Gaels invaded the North (from land they had settled in the South of Ireland). For a thousand years, Antrim and Down successfully resisted this Gaelic expansionist policy spearheaded by the (Northern) O'Neill clan.

The native peoples, facing the imposition of Gaelic rule, finally made their exodus from this half of their Dalriada kingdom to the Scottish half; (Dalriads were, by tradition, descended from 'Riada of the Long Wrist', Chief of Scots); they were evacuated from here, c. 500 A.D., by the Dalriadan chief, Fergus, who is reputed to have carried with him his Antrim crowning stone. The Romans called these Ulstermen the 'Scotti' tribe, and Scottish recorded history acknowledges Fergus as 'the first king of the Scots in Scotland'. Queen Elizabeth 2 traces her ancestry back, through the Stuarts, to Fergus of Dalriada; her Westminster Coronation Stone may be the crowning stone of Fergus which a successor of his took to Scone when the Scotti (or Scots) defeated the Picts; so Ulster, or Dalriada, it appears, is QE2's most ancient realm!

The Celts had their own crowning stones or coronation chairs. Try for yourself the little-known stone seat – 'The Devil's Wishing Chair' – cut into the basaltic face of Carnearny mountain (in a rock outcrop to the left of the forest track which skirts round the front of the Quarry Car Park, at the Lady Hill approach to Tardree Forest). There, where pagan clansmen came to subject themselves to their chieftain (seated upon his inaugural throne), you may look down across the whole of central Ulster to where the land and sky join and you cannot see the birth of one or the death of the other.

It's a nonsense, of course, to speak of 'Antrim' or 'Scotland' or 'Ireland' when discussing ancient times. It was not until the 10th century that the present Scotland was called Scotia, being distinguished from Ireland then as Scotia Minor, while the latter was called Scotia Major.[78] Hence the curious fact, which sounds like an Irishism, that Ireland was the first Scotland, and the first Scotchmen were Irishmen (or, more precisely, Ulstermen; or, more precisely yet again, Antrim-men)!

Meanwhile, back in Antrim, the Celts (or Gaels) were digging-in. The ground they had gone to, in particular, was the superbly fertile Sixmilewater environs; also prime

4

The Devil's Wishing Chair.

choice for such later settlers as the Normans, Elizabethans, Cromwellians and, appropriately, an agricultural 'university' in our own time.

Some 237 Celtic raths and duns (earthen ringworks with surrounding trenches), have been identified in the parishes of Killead and Muckamore; 27 clustered where Muckamore Abbey would later be sited. Rathmore, as we shall see, may probably have been the cause of this unusually high concentration of quality homes; poor Celts did not possess such holdings. The 1,000 years old Spring Farm Rath (J149882; s of Stiles Way) and the complex Ballywee Rath (J218899; 4½ m. ENE of Antrim) are two of the very few raths in State Care.

Raths enclosed a cluster of thatched houses made of mud and timber walls. Cattle, which meant wealth to a bartering Celt, sheltered at night within the rath. 'Fairy forts', they are sometimes called, but they were fortified principally against attacks from wolves and neighbours.

Beneath raths lay one of the keys to the Celts' survival: sophisticated underground chambers (souterrains) served both as secret escape routes and as highly efficient deep-freezes, particularly for milk products. Such souterrains – making unknown the kind of famine which cursed later Irish generations – have been found at Tirgracey, Hurtletoot, Craighall, Rathmore, Lady Hill, Potterswalls and Donegore. Inspect (with a torch), but avoid entering the fine souterrain under the farm lane beside where Parkgate's Grange Road crosses the Four Mile Burn (O.S. map ref: J235885; between the Burn and lane, about 20 yards past the farm gate). 'The Cave', at Bog Head, is Ireland's only known two-chamber, two-storey souterrain.

The story of the Sixmilewater valley is littered with disasters caused when souterrain roofs suddenly collapsed and cattle disappeared; farmers beware when ploughing new ground!

About a quarter of a mile to the north of Rathmore, a large field was discovered entirely honeycombed with networks of souterrains, forming a kind of underground village. An Icelandic legend does tell about Leifr, a pirate, who, while in Ireland, 'there discovered large subterraneous caves, the entrances of which were dark and dismal, but, on entering, he saw the glittering of swords which the men held in their hands'. Those expert cave-hunters, the Vikings, who, the ancient chroniclers said 'left not a cave there underground that they did not explore', simply smoked-out souterrain refugees.

'Finlays Fort' (Rathenraw), must have been the farmstead of particularly wealthy Celts as it had two circular earthen walls and two trenches; a similar and quite dramatically beautiful rath survives at Ballywoodock (to the right of the Connor to Parkgate road). Rathbeg (obliterated by the M2 motorway), had a medieval round-house and a rectangular building with stone foundations (excavated 1967). Archaeologists found a kiln for corn drying, together with iron and stone implements at Rathbeg.

These cyclopean raths, from a close study of ordnance survey maps, appear to have been carefully sited. With intermediate standing stones, they map for us what must have been the ancient line of communication between Connor (with its

5

'cathedral', or abbey), passing between Carnearny and Browndod, to 'Rathmore Castle', (the once royal palace of ancient princes or 'kings' of Dalriada).

> "'Tis called Rathmore, and nothing more know I;
> Illan, belike, has got some old romance,
> Passing with poets for its history . . ."

– from 'Deirdre', Sir Samuel Ferguson.

Rathmore (behind the farm where the Crosskennan Road joins the Greystone Road, a short distance from the M2 Rathbeg roundabout), is an oval ringfort, erected on a basaltic hump, 161 feet across and 16 feet high, with an underground passageway leading down an incredible 428 feet to a well in a large cave. Though its name translates as 'The Great Rath', little, physically, distinguishes it from the 30,000 other raths in Ireland. Except, however, that here resided 'The Great One' – the 'king' of Dalriada.

There is a Celtic claim that the original name was 'Rath-Rogin', and that it was renamed Mor's Rath in memory of she they called Mor who died here of a broken heart when her husband, Breasal, King of Ulster, drowned in Loch Laigh (Belfast Lough). Certainly, in Tighernach's 'Annals' (161 A.D.), there appears the record: 'Breasal, the son of Brian, who reigned in Eamania 19 years, was drowned in Loch Laigh; his spouse, Mor, died of grief; from her Rathmor in Moylinny is named.'

The Rathmore king was obliged to provide a magnificent banquet every seventh year for the High King, whose seat was at Tara:

> "To the King of Rath-Mor-Muigh is due great and kingly wealth; for he is the noblest on the journey, and the first who receives his stipend. Entitled he is, unless he be himself the king of the men of Uladh, to eight hundred cloaks, and two ships, with a bright shield on each shoulder, to a chess-board and white chess-men, eight drinking horns, and eight cups, eight greyhounds, and eight steeds, and eight lances."

('Book of Rights')

The prayers of St Comgall are said to have saved the life of the wife of King Fiachna after she swallowed poison at Rathmore. But the prayers of Ireland's great saint, Columba, cursed one of Rathmore's most celebrated monarchs – King Diarmait mac Cerball.

Diarmait was the last of the great pagan monarchs of Ireland to reside in the ancient palace at Tara. At the time when Ireland was moving from a pagan Iron Age society towards Christianity, Diarmait persisted in celebrating the pagan feast of Tara. When St Ruadan of Lorrha responded by cursing Tara, the royal took the hint and abandoned Tara.

Diarmait was a fiery chieftain: a stolen cow provoked him into war with the king of Connaught, and for stealing a heifer, Diarmait executed his own son. He succeeded to the Dalriadan 'throne' in 565 A.D. by murdering its king, Suibne Araide. As some measure of atonement for this murder, Diarmait fostered Suibne's son, Aedh Dubh, at Rathmore. As the Black Prince of the Dalriadans, Aedh earned a reputation as a mindless murderer. St Columba was outraged when he learned that the founder (Findichan) of Artchain monastery on the island of Tiree, had ordained Aedh into the priesthood. Columba issued a prophetic sentence on both Findichan and Aedh:

> "That right hand, which against the laws of God and the Church, Findichan placed on the head of the son of perdition, shall soon be covered with sores and after much torture, shall precede himself to the grave, and he shall survive the buried hand for many years. But Aedh thus unlawfully ordained, shall return as a dog to his vomit (Prov. xxvi, 11), and he shall again a bloody murder, until at length, pierced in the neck with a spear, he shall fall from a tree into the water and be drowned."

Sure enough, Findichan outlived his right hand which, festering from a blow, had to be amputated (and buried on Ammon Island)!

Meanwhile, Aedh was holed-up at Rathmore, strumming his harp, but all the while secretly hatching a dastardly revenge for his father's murder. Loathe to violate the sacred laws of hospitality, Aedh refused to murder Diarmait in the monarch's own home. You will be glad to hear that he waited until Diarmait left Rathmore to visit a neighbouring knight (Banuan), at Rathbeg ringfort. Then, after surrounding Rathbeg, Aedh set fire to the great round house's thatch. When Diarmait rushed out, Aedh ran his spear through his fiery foster father. As Diarmait fell back into the house, where a heavy rafter collapsed and crushed him to death, perhaps he recalled another of those incredible prophecies handed out by their saints; one he had received many years earlier from St Bec MacDe –

> "It is the hand alone of Aedh Dubh shall convey the draught of death to your lips, in the house of Banban, the knight; and it is the ochtach ('ridge-tree') of the house in which you are, shall fall on your head, after that you have been transfixed by your enemies."

Of such stuff, legends are made.

Diarmait's dying wish was to be buried at the monastery of Clonmacnoise; one of the great Irish centres of holiness and learning, whose foundation stone had been laid by Diarmait. Doubting their ability to shoulder the corpse all the way to central Ireland, however, his attendants decapitated Diarmait; the severed head was carried to Clonmacnoise but the body was buried at nearby Connor, the principal church of the diocese.

And Aedh? In a desperate struggle to retain the kingship he'd inherited, he was wounded in the neck by a spear while aboard a raft on (probably) Lough Neagh, and drowned!

Rathmore became the scene of greater mayhem and murder in 687 A.D. Hostile bands under Egfrid, a Northumbrian king, slew the Dalriadan chief, Cathasagh, 'and a great number of the Irish along with him at the battlefield of Rathmore'. 'The Annals of Innisfallen' record a great meeting of warrior chiefs at Rathmore in 987 A.D. Among those present was the first prince (and later king) of Munster who afterwards became a high-king of Ireland.

Rathmore continued as a 'royal' seat until, at least, the year 1004, when Brian Boru 'marched from Armagh to Rath-more, in Moy-line, until he carried away the hostages of Dalaradia with him'.[80]

St Patrick's Bell Shrine – Courtesy of Ulster Museum.

As well as 'rath', many local placenames preserve the Celtic 'dun': Dunadry (Dun-Eddery) signifies 'the middle fort', perhaps because it was the middle of three Celtic forts on the ancient highway from the celebrated regal hill of Tara to Dunseverick; Dunsilly probably also embraces the name of Sillan, Abbot of Bangor (d.606 A.D.), who once controlled the original monastic settlement of 'old Antrim'.

The arrival of Christianity in this area reminds the present writer of perhaps the most sensational treasure ever found locally: Saint Patrick's Randalstown Bell! The early years of the last century, being the last ones for Henry Mulhollan, the aged schoolmaster of old Edenduffcarrick village (Randalstown), Adam M'Clean was brought to the deathbed of his former teacher. 'The old man requested M'Clean to dig in his garden for an oak box, which contained all that he valued in the world, and which he now bestowed to his friend and former pupil. In the box were found a copy of Bedell's Irish Bible, and the ancient bell called Clog-an-edhachta – "the Bell of the Will (of Patrick)" – of which his ancestors were the hereditary keepers.'[80] The bell's history is well documented in ancient records, the first reference to it appearing in the *Annals of Ulster* under the year 552:

> "I have found what follows in the Book of Cuana. The relics of Patrick were placed in a shrine by Columcille, sixty years after his death. Three precious reliquaries were found in his tomb, to wit the Cup, the Gospel of the Angel, and the Bell of the Will."

Mulhollan's 'oak box' turned out to be the bell-shrine; both bell and shrine were eventually sold to the Royal Irish Academy.

Another ancient manuscript, which advises that St Aengus – who founded the Church of Connor, *c.* 480 A.D. – 'used to sleep with Patrick', prompted Monsignor James O'Laverty of the Royal Irish Academy to observe that 'the story throws a curious light on the domestic arrangements of our forefathers'!

OLD MONASTIC 'ANTRIM'

Gleefully waving his shamrock at the local pagans, Saint Patrick arrived in the early 5th century. As a youth, he had probably passed through here, in chains, on his way to be sold as a slave-shepherd near Slemish.

'I have come among yous to tell yous that there is really only one God, who is actually three Gods, and He wants you to love your enemies!' would have been the jist of what he told our amazed forefathers. History (which in the early times was recorded by monks), doesn't record what the locals told Pat in reply.

The seed which Patrick sowed was to germinate and blossom as Antrim! For the history of the town of Antrim, like many other Irish towns, begins with a church, or monastery. The great monastic house of 'old Antrim' was founded *c.* 495 A.D., just thirty years after Patrick's death.

Aodh is acknowledged by most chroniclers as the founding saint, though Rt. Rev. P. F. Moran makes a strong claim for Durtract, in the editorial notes of *Monasticon Hibernicum* (p. 2).

This Aentrobh – (pronounced 'Entrove') – monastery was situated about thirty yards north and west of where we see the Round Tower (or 'Steeple') today. The foundations of ancient buildings, together with many human remains, were discovered here a little more than a century ago.

Originally, the church would have been made of oak planks and thatched with rushes. Within the perimeter fence (a protection against wolves), would also have been a group of monks' cells made of sticks plastered with mud and thatched, a refectory, kitchen, library and scriptoriam. Undoubtedly there were farm buildings to store fodder and house the animals in winter. The skins of calves (vellum), provided writing materials on which the scribes copied the Gospels or Psalms using quill pens made from goose feathers. It was also a centre of metal working and craftsmanship with its own forge and lime kiln.

Aentrobh (old monastic Antrim).

This ancient church provided two abbots of the historically important University of Bangor: Fintain, 612 A.D., and St Flan, 722 A.D.

Aentrobh (or 'Oentroibh' or 'Entroia') signifies 'the one ridge', so named because the site lay on the western base of a little hilly ridge which wriggled its way from Tardree down to Lough Neagh's Sandy Bay.

The monastic settlement survived attacks from hostile, Gaelic tribes, the great plague of the 660s and repeated assaults by Vikings. When the Norsemen plundered Bangor (822 A.D.), St Comgall's mortal remains and relics were rescued from their shrine and brought to Aentrobh. For six centuries Aentrobh survived until it was (accidentally?) consumed by fire and abandoned in 1147.

THE STEEPLE ENIGMA

Though it has not the romantic setting of its famous counterpart on Fermanagh's Devenish Island, Antrim's classic round tower is older, taller, more accessible, and one of Ireland's finest and rarest of round towers still intact. But what of its origin, date and function?

Scholars have argued seriously that the tower was an astronomical observatory, a centre of druidical festivities, a fire temple, a giant sundial, a phallic symbol or a primitive Buddhist temple! With equal conviction, others have insisted upon a Christian origin, functioning as a baptistery, a burial place, a hermitage or a prison for penitents.

Folk tradition ascribes its building to a 6th century mobile mason – named Goban Saor in ancient tales – or a team of masons specialising in building such towers; originally there seem to have been about ninety round towers scattered across Ireland. Given lime mortar, as used in Antrim's tower – a distinctly Roman technique – Irish builders (used to building in-the-round), might have been able to erect such architecturally sophisticated, free-standing structures any time from the

9

The Round Tower, Antrim.

arrival of monks from W. Europe/post-Roman Britain in the 6th century.

In a hostile, pagan country, the early monasteries would have needed an impregnable refuge for both personnel and valuables; five Irish towers – including the one on Ram's Island in Lough Neagh – were destroyed by pagan-Irish tribes. Records show that Antrim's monastery was 'spoiled' in 1018 by 'the men of Fermanach' and by 'the men of Tyrone' in 1030.

Although the monastery's most-valuable possession was its founding-saint's bell, perhaps the old-Irish description of these towers as 'cloc tees' (bell-houses) alludes, some have argued, to a monastic custom of laying claim to the possessions of any stranger dying within the sound of the church bell? In this extensively forested environment, the sound of the bell would carry further from the top of a tower! A light at the four upper windows could shine out the welcome over the tree tops to guide travellers to the house of safety, rest and love at this important ancient crossroads.

Just as magnificent cathedrals create an appropriate sense of awe, a lofty stone finger-tower, pointing symbolically to the heavens, would produce a similar psychological impression on the imaginations of unskilled – (building solely in wood) – pagan Celts?

Its context is certainly Christian. However, no evidence exists – in archaeology or ancient manuscript – to justify dating our round tower earlier than the 7th century. Most probably, the tower was built by Aentrobh monks in the 9th or early 10th centuries, in response to the piratical Viking raids which commenced in the 800s.

Five years after their assaults on Bangor, the Vikings infested Lough Neagh, establishing a base for operations (against Antrim and Muckamore) at Mainwater Foot. ('Ulster' is the Norse form of 'The Place of the Men of Ulad'.) Monks would be warned of an invader's approach by the bell of the sentinel, stationed on lookout at the upper four windows (which face the cardinal points of the compass), under the cone (93 ft aloft). A (rope) ladder would have been used to reach the tower's narrow entrance door, 7 ft above ground level; (lowering the surrounding land to today's level has now exposed the offsets of the foundations). With the ladder hauled up behind them, the heavy oak door slammed shut, and with a goodly supply of big boulders (to drop, as missiles, from the bell-loft), plus emergency rations of food and water always kept within, the monks and their monastic valuables were safe; by such a method, the traditional artistic and religious Irish culture was preserved through the Dark Ages.

It is thought that the stone which forms the inside lintel of the door was brought from Sandy Brae, near Doagh. An oak beam (still visible) was inserted between it and the outside lintel, giving the wall here a thickness of 3'9". Tapering gracefully, at the summit the wall is just 1'8" thick. The holes in the wall, inside, where joists would have rested, confirm that there was a spiral staircase, a landing place at each window, and six floors.

Bullaun Stone ('The Witches Stone') – Courtesy of Ulster Museum.

Most of the tower is built with basalt stones brought from Tardree. The original (octagonal?) cone was granite – and crowned with a stone spear – but this was shattered by lightning in 1819. At that time, Tardree stone was used by William Clarke (of Steeple House) to reset the cone, but for the capstone he made use of the preserved stone lintel of old Aentrobh's church. The date of the stemmed, ringed cross, carved in relief above the doorway is unknown. (Part of an ancient shrine found at this site was donated in 1835 to the Ulster Museum.) The timber window frames are modern.

The WITCHES STONE at the base of the tower was originally sited 120 yards to the north. The two holes ground into the surface of this giant bullaun stone – reputed never to be without water – made for Aentrobh's monks a kitchen table of sorts where grain could be washed (using the larger hole), with water from the nearby stream and ground in the smaller hole.

Nonetheless, as recently as the last century, many Antrim folk firmly contended that the town's name was originally that of a witch who was so annoyed at the erection of the tower that, having squatted on the construction site, and the tower erected beneath her, she fell from the summit to this 'Witches Stone', leaving in it those imprints of her knee and elbow! Old Ann Trim?

It was 17th century Presbyterian Scots settlers who first recognised and christened Antrim's round tower as 'The Steeple' of some auld kirk.

Stations and penances were made from the tower in former times to the HOLY WELL, to the north (a short distance above the present Steeple Road-Stiles Way intersection). Local tradition that the well's water possessed healing properties, (though the water was slightly chalybeate) is clearly not the derivation of 'Holywell'.

MUCKAMORE ABBEY

Like some of his followers, Saint Patrick was a genius when it came to prophecies. When Patrick arrived at Mach aire Mor ('the great field of adoration') where druids were reputed to conduct religious rites, our patron saint was of the opinion that 'a certain child of life, called Colmanellus, will build a church and will gather together here many sons of life and many fellow-citizens of the angels'. More than a hundred years later (in 555) Colmanellus was born, and guess what? He built Muckamore Abbey just where Patrick said he would! Even more impressive is the fact that he had it built by the year 550! (St Columbkille [Colmanellus' uncle] had acquired the site from the eldest son of Rathmore's murdered Diarmait).

At first, Colmanellus was probably a solitary teacher of religious studies in small cells at Muckamore though later it appears that this monastery developed into an important seminary of learning where 200-300 Augustinian students most probably studied the seven liberal arts – the 'trivium' of grammar, rhetoric and dialectic and the 'quadrivium' of arithmetic, geometry, astronomy and music – though the expounding of Holy Scripture remained the heart of all teaching. (Extracts from the register of one of Muckamore's priors are preserved in the British Museum).[83]

The abbey extended from about 390 yards along the left bank of the Sixmilewater and 160 yards south to the graveyard and to Muckamore House. One of its three-feet thick walls still forms a useful boundary to the garden of Muckamore House; the presence of Pitch-stone Porphy suggests the building materials were brought from Carnearny Hill.

The Vikings destroyed the original abbey. What appalling scenes of brutality and horror must have been enacted here. It is said that the abbey which John De Courcy's Normans rebuilt and rededicated to Ss. Mary and Colman was destroyed during Edward Bruce's 14th century invasion, but rebuilt again. It was certainly going strong again at the start of the 15th century when the largest and most important of Ulster's annual horse fairs were presented at the abbey under licence from Henry 7. Henry 8, however, dissolved the monasteries of his realm and Muckamore was robbed of its abbey, lands and churches: 'the eight townlands of the priory being Ballymackemair, Ballyshane, Ochyll, Ballow, Tearogearye, Ballylaghe, Ballyestiene, and of the manor etc. of Massereene the town parish of Ballymohellan, two townlands near the woods of Dunmore and Kilwooderag, and of the said woods, and of all the tithes in lower Clandeboy, and two parts of the tithes in eight parishes or granges in upper Clandeboy, two parts of the tithes of Magherscergan in the Reuts, and of Kilglarne in the Ardes, the rectory of Whitekirk, in Island Magee and the tithes of a quarter of land called Carrownaghan in the county of Down'.[9] (The ruins of a little priory at Rathmore [founded 1251?] survived until the present century.)

The land about the abbey being so very fertile, the O'Neills named it Magh-Comair (Muckamore): 'the plain of the confluence' of the Sixmilewater and the Clady Water; a case of there being more muck here than anywhere else?

However, there is a not-totally-unrelated Gaelic orthography – 'Mach-airi-mor', meaning 'the great field of adoration', which suggests that Muckamore could have been of Druidical importance as a place of worship.

The old abbey and its lands, as we shall see later, were granted by James I to the Langford family of Devon. From that time forward, Muckamore bore a distinctly English character and provided a noticeable southern frontier for the Mid-Antrim Scots accents.

Today, a stroll along the beautiful Moylena Banks Riverside Walk will bring the visitor to Muckamore Abbey's charming parklands and admirable hospital for the handicapped.

THE MIRACULOUS STONES OF CRANFIELD

The practice of counting prayers on beads, as introduced into Ireland by St Patrick, originated three miles west of Randalstown on the northern shores of Lough Neagh!

That was the conclusion of Rev. James O'Laverty's research in 1884. He was attracted to the site of Cranfield Church on learning that one of the most ancient church practices – counting prayers by stones or pebbles – was traditionally performed at 'that miraculous spring which is near the Church of Creamchoill' ('the wood of wild garlic' – Cranfield).

Holy pilgrimages were made to Cranfield every May 1st when 'Cranfield pebbles' were sought to protect women during childbirth, men from drowning and homes from fire or burglary.

Holy Well, Cranfield – Courtesy of Ulster Museum.

Richardson, in his *Great Folly of Pilgrimages* (1727), tells us:—

> "At Cranfield, in the County of Antrim, there is a south-running spring of common water, said to be consecrated by St Colman, a famous Irish saint. Pilgrims go to it on May eve; they empty and clear the well in the twilight, stay all night about it, saying a certain numbers of Paters, Aves and Credos. In the morning, they find small transparent stones, of an amber colour, in the bottom of the well, which (if you believe them) grew there the night before, and will preserve those that carry one of them about them from any loss by fire or water. These stones are to be found there at any time yet the natives thereabouts will not be convinced of it."

O'Laverty went in search of the ice-clear holy pebbles in July and engaged a local boy and girl to empty the well for him. The young girl scraped the bottom of the well and produced, with each handful of gravel, two or three of the stones. Surveying the 'dark green rotten mouldering rocky ground' of the area between the well and the lough, O'Laverty concluded that 'especially in dry weather, when the lough rises not too high or the well be not over-pressed with water from the upper grounds, and that they are in the rock, and rise as that is broken or raised'.

The pebbles, not unique to Cranfield, are amber-coloured crystals of gypsum.

St Colman's Well, according to another tradition, was blessed with healing properties by St Olcan, who reputedly lies buried at Cranfield's 13th century church (nearby) in earth brought from Rome. So it was deemed a doubly holy place, and records show that the pilgrims who visited there walked barefoot thirteen times around the church, thirteen times around the well, drank from the well and, finally, bathed in it.

In more recent times, pilgrims would collect seven ordinary stones to count 'the rounds'. Then, on any three consecutive days between May Eve (old date) and June 29, they would kneel at the tiny door of the church saying 'Our Father', 'Hail Mary' and 'I Believe in God', recite the prayers of the Rosary of the Blessed Virgin, slowly circle the church ruins and drop one stone at the door each time. After seven rounds of the church, seven more stones were collected for seven rounds of the well.

> "It is probable that in former ages, instead of the common stones now used, the Cranfield Pebbles, which were then more easily procured, were used for counting the prayers, and hence they obtained the sacred character with which, in popular estimation, they are invested."[80]

We know from Palladius (writing in the 4th century), of an abbot who faithfully recited the Lord's Prayer three hundred times daily and kept track of the number by dropping pebbles into his lap. 'So it would seem,' concluded O'Laverty, 'the Cranfield Pebbles are the original Beads as introduced by St Patrick.'

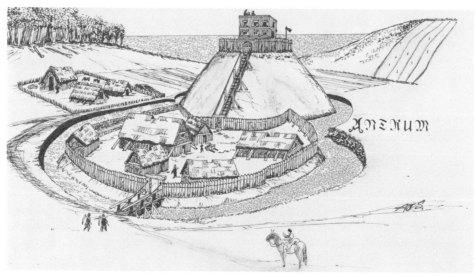

Antrum (Anglo-Norman Antrim).

THE BIRTH OF 'ANTRUM'

While some Vikings were calculating how to flush monks out of Irish round towers, their Norse brothers had invaded and settled in France. French-Vikings' descendants – Normans (from Normandy, 'the land of the Northmen') – successfully invaded England in 1066. These Anglo-Norman conquerors were implored (and indeed bribed) by an Irish chieftain to invade Ireland in the 12th century.

Following the abandonment of old Aentrobh in 1147, the Sixmilewater valley generally had become an area of Gaelic-Irish pastoralism. But thirty years later it had to contend with venturous, young Norman freebooters.

The Sixmilewater valley, eminently suitable for the intense agricultural productivity of Anglo-Norman settlers, was organised and settled by 1226. The territory was part of their bailiwick of Antrum (which emerges as County Antrim in the 1333 inquisition).

With a trained eye for country, all about our district the Normans constructed their distinctive steep-sided plum-pudding-like mounds ('mottes'), each crowned with a wooden archery tower (or 'bretasche') effectively combining defence and domesticity.

Trenches were dug around both the base of each motte and its adjacent open space (or 'bailey'). Rathenraw still has its splendid motte and bailey. The Normans adapted Donegore's prehistoric burial mound to serve as a motte, and built another at the east end of Rathmore. At Muckamore they constructed a motte with a crescentic bailey, and a motte-and-bailey with stone revetted ditches in the Massereene Deerpark. Across the 'Abhann na bhfeagacha' (Sixmilewater) they probably constructed a wooden bridge near where the Forum's 'Leisure Lap' commences today; here, where the river could best be forded (in summer), John De Courcy erected the principal motte-and-bailey, which was to give its name to the entire bailiwick or county.

The Anglo-Normans called the place 'Antrum', which, like 'Aentrobh', signifies that 'one ridge' winding down to Lough Neagh from Tardree. De Courcy called the motte he built beside the river – which is known today as the 'Mound' in the Castle Grounds – his 'Castle of Antrum'.

The Account Rolls of Elizabeth de Burgh (1353-60) offer a glimpse of 'Antrum villae': a castle, court, tower, orchards, brewers, corn mills, and 'a cow sold for

4s. 6d'. The pre-eminent family of the bailiwick (with a base upon Donegore) were the Savages (who provided sheriffs for Twescard and seneschals for Ulster); the Logans were the principal rentiers of the Sixmilewater valley, with charters from De Courcy, De Lacy and De Burgh and were of such nobility as to be attending Parliament in 1310.

King John established control of Lough Neagh with a fleet of two galleys. Muckamore Abbey was restored and endowed by De Courcy. The 'Grange' (of Nilteen, or Muckamore) was their old-French term (derived from Latin, meaning 'a barn'), which the Norman-English applied to areas where they successfully established their feudal pattern of mixed farming. Massereene (south of the Sixmilewater) and, north of the river, Upper Antrum, and beyond it Lower Antrum, became three of the bailiwick's (county's) fourteen baronies, (which term derives from the Norman-English barons). Antrim town is in the Barony of Upper Antrim though Antrim parish, on the southern border of Upper Antrim, is partly in the Barony of Upper Toome. The 'Manor' (of Moylinny, for example) signified an area successfully conquered and controlled by a castle; the Manor of Rathmore was granted by King Edward to his knight, Sir Robert Savage. Savage's castle probably stood in the townland of Ballysavage, near Parkgate.

Incidentally, but importantly, should the modern mania for using rural road names in postal addresses succeed, we shall be the poorer for the loss of our expressive townland names. Consider Parkgate, for example: diocese of Connor, manor of Moylinny, barony of Upper Antrim and townland of Durhamsland, in the parish of Donegore, and Moyadam in the Grange of Nilteen. What a cost when such is lost. How many of the original 'Sixteen towns of Antrim' do you recognise? – Ballygallantrim, Ballycrigiderrie, Ballyconnagh, Ballywinevise, Ballyneeregy, Ballyberan, Ballyramull, Ballyrathbeg, Ballymullen, Ballycroskenan, Ballytollynandolly, Ballygaltiwinsie, Ballyantrim, Ballykeile, Ballynormullen and Ballynelagrenbeg.

By the 14th century, Antrum, (with its County Court), had been replaced (by Dunadry) as the county's principal manorial centre. But the Castle of Antrum still remained firmly in the hands of (De Mowbray) English barons.

With green songs seething on their lips and vengeance in their hearts, the good Clann Aedha Buidhe – (the 'Clanaboy' or Clandeboy) – O'Neills waited west of the Bann, where the English could or would not go; waiting for an opportune moment to retake the territories they had originally taken when they first invaded Ulster.

ANTRIM KINGS AND QUEENS

The O'Neills' revenge upon the English began, ironically, in the shape of a massive Scots' invasion (1315) by Bannockburn veterans, led by Edward Bruce (brother of Robert). Bruce received from the O'Neill chief his title 'King of Ulster and heir to the whole of Ireland'.

Before defeating in battle the Earl of Ulster's principal Norman garrison (at our diocese's 'cathedral city' of Connor), Bruce overran the Normans' motte-castle at Rathmore, after winning the bloody battle fought in the adjacent 'Castle Field'. The Savage family was forced to flee south where they settled on the Ards peninsula. The O'Neills were greatly encouraged. (Savage's mail-clad and iron-helmeted knights and archers had, with lances and swords, slain three thousand Irish, the latter being clad in peasant dress and armed only with axes and slings. The battlefield is reputed to have been in the valley between Rathmore and Donegore.) The O'Neills attacked Antrum and expelled the De Mowbrays; by 1370 they had consolidated their power in Mid-Antrim.

If this is supposed to mark the Normans' exit from our narrative, the last laugh must be theirs for by making in-laws of the Irish they have produced, for example, Fitzgeralds for the South of Ireland and, today, the Earl of Ulster stands just thirteenth in the order of succession to the British Crown. Even after the Scots' and Gaelic-Irish' 'expulsion' of the English, the farming receipts from 'Antrum villae' show a constantly rising trend.

The Barony of Antrum reverted in name to the O'Neills' 'Masaregna' (Masarine), signifying 'The Queen's Hill'; commemorating one of their clan's queens who drowned in the Sixmilewater. There was, of course, no 'town' of Antrim yet; the only settlements recognisable as towns were Carrickfergus and Newry.

Masarine held scattered villages of straw and mud huts where the people slept on rushes spread on the ground. They kept themselves warm with tight leggings and short, loose coats of very coarse goatshair or the O'Neills' distinctive saffron-coloured linen. Women wore only a chemise and a blanket with a linen headscarf tied in front.

On this south side of the river and about 100 yards west of our Massereene Bridge, 15th century O'Neills founded the (3rd Order) Franciscan friary of the Brothers of Masarine ('Castlemonybray'), and endowed it with thirty acres stretching south along the lough shore.

But the days of saints and scholars were long past. With her eye on the dangerous behaviour of the Northern O'Neills and the other eye admiring the great virgin oak forests and potential farmlands of Ulster, the Queen of England resolved to launch a determined war to take control of the Province. It was a policy (whose repercussions are still being felt) which would plant a new town in the Sixmilewater valley and where Norman-English ancestors had found the river could be easily forded. The 'Owen-a-view' ('river of the rushes') as it now was, was about to become the Six-Mile Water.

ANTHRONA

The poet, Sir Philip Sidney was the preux chevalier of the Elizabethan age, but his father – Sir Henry Sidney – as far as the Irish were concerned, was one whose name was writ in water, if not in blood. After wreaking havoc among those loyal to the rebellious (and most Shakespearean Irish-Macbeth) Shane The Proud O'Neill, Sir Henry, as Lord Deputy, renamed Lough Neagh – Lough Sidney! But ochanee a nee oh, nobody liked the name because Sidney couldn't attract settlers to the wild Ulster thought to be half way to North America and half or maybe more of the way to the North Pole.

Though the ill-starred Earl of Essex (who led an expedition here in 1573 to conduct a merciless campaign against the O'Neills) was removed from office in disgrace, among his officers who remained at their Carrickfergus base was Devon's young Cpt. Hugh Clotworthy.

Clotworthy received orders to march his troops six miles across the countryside in the direction of Ballyboley Mountain where they would encounter the Water, or river (and hence the Elizabethan name, 'Six-Mile Water') which led down to the Vale of Moylinny and to Masarine.

By 1596, where the Sixmilewater could be forded at Masarine, the Elizabethan English had created their small settlement of Anthrona (signifying 'a ford or ferry'). The parish church (All Saints') still sports the 1596 datestone. 'Gall-Antrum' (the Antrum or Antrim of the English foreigner), the O'Neills dubbed the place.

Hugh Clotworthy supervised the construction of secure military quarters beside the old Norman motte (which site would later display the elegant stone Castle of

Antrim). A contemporary account tells us:

> "At Masarine there is a little forte built in the midst of the river with fair timber houses built by Captain Hugh Clotworthy, covered with good shingle together with necessary houses for stores and munition. The forte is fenced with rampier of earth and strong palisado round about it, with a deep broad ditch and drawbridge over it."

With Masarine securely garrisoned, ammunition, men and provisions could be brought from Carrickfegus and shipped across the great frontier of Lough Neagh to Mountjoy in Tyrone and Charlemont at the Blackwater. But the O'Neills were determined the Queen's writ wouldn't run west of the lough or the Bann. Repeatedly, they swept across the lough and sailed their light curraghs right up the Sixmilewater in hit-and-run attacks on Clotworthy's fort.

Perhaps Clotworthy accompanied Sir John Chichester's three hundred soldiers who attacked and burned Edendow Carreck (Shane's Castle, Randalstown) in 1597, and captured the Castle of Toome. He certainly helped that other swash-buckling Elizabethan Chichester adventurer, Sir Arthur, to build (for £721 5s. 1¼d.) a Lough Neagh navy. Of a thirty-tonner, Chichester wrote to the Queen:

> "I have launched the great boat and twice visited Tyrone with her . . . we have killed, burned, and spoiled all along the Lough shore above one hundred people of all sorts . . . we spare none of what quality or sex soever, and it hath bred much terror in the people."

This was tough, frontier warfare such as the Elizabethans were also directing against the North American Indians. Both the Indians and the O'Neills of Ulster often gave as good as they received. But as well as acknowledging that there were atrocities committed on both sides, the record isn't totally damning: Walter Deveraux, 1st Earl of Essex, invested nearly all of his private fortune attempting to plant settlers in this area; when Chichester overran the important and grand O'Neill fort at Inishnoughan (site unknown today), in the ancient forest of Killultagh, the English discovered their 'primitive Irish savages' quietly and successfully cultivating fields of good corn.

Victory came for the English in 1603 with the submission of the great Gaelic chieftain (and Renaissance prince), Hugh O'Neill. Chichester was rewarded with confiscated O'Neill territories and charged with asserting the supremacy of Church and State for which task he was appointed Lord Deputy. There would be a United Ireland for the first time in history. And peace? Now it's a truth universally acknowledged that the lion shall lie down with the calf but the calf won't get much sleep.

As Admiral of Lough Neagh, Chichester prudently decided to maintain his naval power with Hugh Clotworthy as the 'sea' captain stationed at Anthrona. Clotworthy, who was also appointed High Sheriff of County Antrim and granted Masarine, was one of four Elizabethan officers to be knighted (1617) and locally settled.

Sir Fulke Conway acquired (1610) the lands of Killultagh and Derryvolgie; Sir Roger Langford – who had been left in charge at Killultagh after the fall of Inishnoughan – was confirmed (1622) as the possessor of Muckamore's old abbey and 400-acre demesne; and Sir Robert Norton commenced erecting Castle Robin, near Lisburn, and Norton Castle, at Templepatrick, but sold the latter to another of Essex's captains – Henry Upton – and took as his wife a daughter of Sir Hugh Clotworthy.

LADY MARIAN'S WOLFHOUND

When the old Gaelic order collapsed after the 'Flight of the Earls', and Sir Hugh Clotworthy had secured (1613) his little stone-built artillery fort (or 'castle'-keep) – sited opposite Masarine Abbey (the present Antrim Forum site) – complete with a menacing canon fixed in position on the summit of the adjacent old Norman motte, he brought his beautiful young bride, Sir Roger Langford's daughter – 'Marian of the tresses' – to Masarine (Anglicised to 'Massereene').

'After the first few months of fondest endearment were over, Marian began to feel that the bawn – for the castle was not then erected – made a dreary abode. She missed in that interminable and solitary wood, the gaities of the Rock (Carrickfergus Castle), her early companions, and the old familiar scenes of Island Magee, the Green-Isle and Lough Morne. Captain Hugh himself was frequently absent on dangerous services which his position imposed.'

Marian often whiled away her lonely hours by wandering through the woods to the lough's edge. There exists a most dramatic account of one of her afternoon walks which took her to the mouth of the Sixmilewater:

'Startled by a sharp growl she turned round, when, horror-struck, she beheld a huge wolf, with distended jaws and eyes of fire, in the act of springing upon her from the thicket. Uttering a scream of terror she fell to the ground. Her weakness saved her life: the wolf missing his deadly spring fell, and rolled beyond her. Almost instantaneously another roar was heard, still louder than the first, and a second animal swept with lightning speed across her and seized the wolf. In the fearful noise and conflict of the two ferocious animals fighting and tearing each other over her prostrate form she swooned. How long she remained insensible she never knew, but on regaining consciousness, she saw the wolf stretched out on the bank, at some distance, mangled and dead, and lying by her side licking her hand was an Irish wolf-dog, panting and wounded. The animal had saved her life and killed his natural enemy. The Lady Marian, with gratitude and a woman's tenderness, had the suffering animal conveyed to the bawn and tended with care.

One day, after he had recovered, the dog disappeared in the direction of Massereene Abbey. Some considerable time elapsed. The castle was erected, and the incident of the wolf and the Irish wolf-dog was forgotten by all but the Lady Marian.

One of those sudden, squally storms from the lough, which are so frequent in that district, came on at the close of a dreary winter's day. Night suddenly descended, the lightning ceased, succeeded by an unbroken and impenetrable darkness. High over the wind as it came in its headlong course, roaring and crashing through the woods, the deep baying of a wolf dog was heard. Round and round the walls of the castle it sounded its warning tones.

Startled by an incident so unusual, the warders, by the direction of Sir Hugh, sprang to the Mound (i.e. old motte). Hastily lighting their turf and bogwood beacon-fire, they saw by the glare of the light a dark mass of the Irish enemy, armed with matchlock, pike and skein, and bearing some rude scaling ladders. A round shot from Roaring Tatty, the long gun on the Mound, and a sharp fusilade from the bastions on their flank, rapidly dispersed the foe, and preserved the castle and its inmates from danger.

But what of the wolf-dog? Before the enemy left, a howling cry of pain was heard accompanied by a few shots.

In the grey dawn of the morning, as the warders went forth upon their round of inspection, they found amidst fallen leaves a stream of blood at the grand entrance gate, and some flattened musket balls by the wall side. But, most singular of all, on looking up towards the roof of the castle, they beheld, standing on the highest turret, the wolf-dog himself, perfect in every limb, as he left the Lady Marian some time before, but transformed now into solid stone.'[52]

Sir Hugh, it appears, had a stone model made of the hound – its ears pricked, muzzle lifted, teeth bared in warning – and astutely took advantage of the commotion to climb up to the castle's roof to mount it on one of the four front towers. Presumably he recognised the potential it might have in warding off hostile but superstitious Irish.

During later alterations to the castle, the stone hound was transferred to the grounds' perimeter wall, where the blood and musket balls had been found. 'So long as it remains there,' runs an old tradition, 'so long will the Massereene family continue to prosper. But when it falls, then, alas! . . . for the family will speedily decay.'

It's a good story. The truth may be a different story, however, as tales of wolfhounds-killing-wolves have a very ancient pedigree in Ireland.

But one Clotworthy who wasn't afraid of any big bad wolf figures in history's most-reliable record discovered to date concerning the destruction of the last wolf in Ireland: *A Compendious System of Chronology,* written in 1823 by Belfast schoolmaster, J. Compton, quotes a record dated 1692: 'The last wolf seen in Ireland is killed with Irish wolf-dogs on the hill of Aughnabrack, near Belfast, by Clotworthy Upton, of Castle-Upton, Templepatrick.' Aughnabrack, signifying 'the hill of the wolf', is still known as Wolf Hill (West Belfast).

THE 'PLANTATION' OF ANTRIM

'King James 1, having given some lands to some men whom he had nobilitated, these men sought tenants for their lands; and from Scotland came many.' Though Antrim (and Down) were never part of the official Plantation of Ulster (1609), royal patents granting rights to hold fairs and markets (as early as 1605 in Antrim town) had attracted 'adventurous spirits, from Scotland, whose finances had run low, glad of the opportunity of a chance in a new country; new, yet within sight of the old'.[78] With the encouragement of men like Clotworthy and Chichester, many of these 'adventurous' Scots settled in Antrim, erecting clusters of thatched cottages among other Scots who had created a 'Scotch Quarter' (now Church Street) as early as the 1590s. (Crumlin Pres. church, although an 1839 structure, sports a plaque inscribed – 'Ecclesia Scotica'.)

As the early years of the 17th century rolled on, the state of affairs in Scotland grew more and more uncomfortable, especially for those who wished to enjoy the simple forms, the pure doctrine of Presbyterianism. Many were glad to escape to a land which promised them rest and immunity from persecution. Among them came the Agnews, Becks, Boyds, Campbells, Crawfords, Fergusons, Orrs and Sloans: weavers, glovers, bakers, pewterers, chandlers, tanners, nailers, millers and 'malsters'. Antrim's non-urban pastoral landscape was significantly changed.

Some of these Protestant settlers, however, were aliens only by speech, not by birth or religion. They were, it seems, more Irish than the (Gaelic) Irish: they were, I've heard it whispered, lineal descendants of the old Antrim Dalriads who had been driven across the North Channel by Celtic invasion and expansionism eleven centuries before! Further, the 17th century's learned Bishop Ussher of Armagh, in his *Discourse on the Religion anciently professed by the Irish,* examined in detail how the comparatively pure form of Christianity originally introduced here by St Patrick (and castigated by Pope Honorius for its non-conformity to Rome), disappeared with the 6th century expulsion of the Dalriada people to reappear only with the return of the 17th century lowland Presbyterian Scots, particularly those who 'came homing' to the valley of the Sixmilewater!

The Antrim-Scot aborigine was certainly a very interesting man. (And she is not at all uninteresting either.) Those who would claim descent (which, politically, would be a very interesting situation today), might first reflect that their ancestral natives were thick-skinned, short and probably fat, ignorant pagans. Ulster's 'madness' probably stems from the fact that on Day 1 they found themselves sailing south up the north-flowing Bann and then north up the parallel but south-flowing river Maine!

Antrim attracted some of the first of the Lowland Scottish Presbyterian and English Puritan preachers. Shortly after the first Presbyterian ministry was begun (at Broadisland, Ballycarry, in 1613, by Rev. Edward Brice whose grave and church ruins still remain), John Knox's grandson – Rev. Josias Welsh – came as personal chaplain to Captain Upton (Castle Upton) at Templepatrick; Welsh's grave is clearly marked in front of Templetown Mausoleum. To Donegore (Pres. ch. founded 1627) came Rev. Andrew Stewart, whose son would write the (incomplete) history of the Calvanistic Church of Ireland. (St John's, Donegore, 'is said to be of ancient erection and to have been used successively by Roman Catholics, Protestants of the Church of England, Presbyterians and again by members of the Church of England in whose possession it now is' [O.S. Donegore Memoir].) Oldstone parish was put in the charge of a refugee preacher from St Andrews, the eccentric James Glendinning, who 'though poor in scholarship and rather unstable, having a great voice and vehement delivery he roused up the people of Antrim and awakened them with terror'. (The first Antrim Presbyterian congregation, formed by 1619, remains one of the oldest in Ireland.)

There was little evidence of Christianity among the early 'adventurous' settlers, so the various Protestant preachers launched a Great Revival (at Oldstone) in 1625, and the Sixmilewater Valley became known as 'the cradle of Irish Presbyterianism'. Local bard, William McComb, writing in 1842, celebrated the memory of the Revival in his verse:

"Two hundred years ago, the dew of God's refreshing power
On Oldstone and on Antrim fell, like Israel's manna shower;
The waters of the Six-Mile stream flowed rapidly along,
But swifter far the Spirit passed o'er the awakened throng:
Where'er the fruitful river went, God's presence seemed to go,
And thus the Spirit blessed our sires, two hundred years ago."

Novel monthly meetings were conducted in Antrim on the first Friday of each month. Such meetings were to establish Antrim as a presbyterial centre, and, later, the meeting place for the original General Synods. In those pioneering days, of course, there was no official 'Presbyterian Church of Ireland'.

The parish church (All Saints'), was the fourth planters' church in Ireland and is currently the second oldest. The celebrated Puritan English vicar, John Ridge, was its first-recorded (1619) preacher. 'He used not to have many points in his sermons,' records reveal, 'but he so enlarged those he had that it was scarcely possible for any hearer to forget his preaching.' Before the disappearance of Episcopalian toleration towards Presbyterian dissenters, John Ridge welcomed both Anglican and Presbyterian worshippers into the parish church. A Revivalist of 1625, Ridge refused to sign Episcopalian canons in accordance with the Order of Convocation and was eventually ejected from his pulpit by Bishop Leslie, who said of him: 'The Church hath no need of those who do not know how to obey her.' Nonetheless, Protestant worship with revivalist tendencies was strongly supported by Sir Hugh and Lady Marian Clotworthy of the little stone fortress they called their 'Castle of Antrim', erected between 1610 and 1613 (beside where, in 1662, a castle-proper – such as we see in old photographs – was erected).

To help solve the chronic unemployment situation in Antrim, Sir Hugh Clotworthy turned to his native Devonshire. In Exeter he persuaded Robert Wreyford, a fuller (cloth merchant), to accept a grant (1632) of six acres at (Riverside?) Antrim and establish a fulling trade. Knowing nothing of Devon's River Wrey, Antrim folk were delighted to welcome their new 'Master Reford'. Under his son, Lewis, the business expanded to make the Refords of Antrim one of Ulster's great linen families.

As far away as Kells-Water Lewis Reford opened a mill, and established the 84 acre Moylinny Farme at Antrim and his Spring Farme just north of George Jackson's Steeple lands.

The 1745 map of Spring Farme's 76 acres shows the Reford mansion beautifully sited between the (walled?) garden and the orchard, with (as so many of the great local houses had) a south-westerly aspect affording panoramic views of Lough Neagh. Immediately in front of the great house was its 'Bleach yard' with parkland beyond; the 'Broad Meddow field' to the south; and the 'Spring field' among several to the north, before the marshy edge of the estate which marked the beginning of Houston's farm and the lands of Francis Campbell and Joseph McKay.

Lewis Reford was one of this country's early Quakers. The first meeting of what became the Society of Friends in Ireland was held (1653) in Reford's Antrim house by local businessman, William Edmundson (brother of an English soldier at Antrim Castle). Said John Wesley, during a visit to Antrim and after reading the *Journal* of Edmundson (the founder of Ireland's Society of Friends): 'His opinions I leave; but what a spirit was there! Could mistakes send such a man as this to Hell? Not so. I am so far from believing this that I scruple not to say – "Let my soul be with the soul of William Edmundson!"' (A few Moravians had their own meeting-house in the back garden of 21 Church Street.)

The worst of the religious intolerance and persecution of the 17th century came in the decades after Sir Hugh Clotworthy died in 1630 and was interred in Antrim Parish Churchyard. He was succeeded by his elder son, John.

THE FIRST LORD MASSEREENE

Sir John Clotworthy, first Lord Massereene and Baron of Lough Neagh, married Margaret, eldest daughter of the first Viscount Ranelagh, Sir Roger Jones. The story of his experiences supports the contemporary description of him as 'a man of simple and temperate habits, great capacity, courteous manners, unflinching courage, a staunch and loyal friend, a good hater and bitter enemy'. Though he represented the county of Antrim in the old Irish Parliament, he could do little about the bishops who were intolerant of such nonconformist Puritan vicars as Antrim's John Ridge.

On behalf of the monarch, Charles 1, Archbishop Laud directed that all pastors who would not conform to Episcopacy should be deposed and put on trial. From his deathbed, Stewart of Donegore sensed the trouble ahead: 'Woe to thee, Donegore, for the nettles and the long grass shall be in greater plenty in thee than ever were people to hear the Word of God.'

The vicar of Antrim and four of the other principal revivalists were removed (1636) from office by the Bishop of Down. Ridge's successor in the pulpit of Antrim's parish church was the rector of Ahoghill who, in his turn, suffered the persecution of imprisonment.

The darkest days of persecution arrived when Charles installed Thomas Wentworth (known later as the Earl of Strafford) as his Lord Deputy of Ireland. Wentworth was determined to establish the royal authority and make Ireland contribute handsomely to Charles' treasury. He drove up rents and claimed customs duties. When he made linen yarns a monopoly, Massereene protested loudly. As patron of Antrim's nonconformists, Massereene had already petitioned for the abolition of Episcopal ascendancy. Lord Deputy Wentworth retaliated with threats to take possession of the Castle of Antrim.

Then came the 'Black Oath', which obliged all dissenters to swear allegiance to Charles, obey all his future commands and renounce the Scottish (Presbyterian) National Covenant. (The founder of the Scots Covenanters in Ireland is supposed to have been Parkgate preacher, Alexander Peden.) Among the thousands who resisted the Oath, the 'lucky' ones suffered years of incarceration in filthy dungeons. The notorious Star Chamber court delivered countless sentences of high treason. Sir Robert Adair was indicted of high treason, had his Ballymena property confiscated and was obliged, like many fellow Presbyterians, to seek refuge in Scotland. Others fled to Holland or tried to emigrate west across the North Atlantic to the American colonies. Wentworth went so far as to specially prepare ships to help them on their way.

Massereene resigned his seat in the Irish Parliament and fled with his wife to England where he was elected to represent the boroughs of Maldon, Essex, and

Bossiney (Cornwall) in the House of Commons (the 'Long Parliament'). His mother, Dame Marian, who remained in Antrim to manage the Massereene estate, was summoned before the Court of High Commission in Dublin to answer for her nonconformity. But in England, her son had seized an opportunity which would give him the power to destroy Wentworth.

As soon as the Long Parliament met, Lord Massereene raised the issue of Wentworth's conduct in governing Ireland and seconded Pym's motion that the Lord Deputy be impeached. The action was wholly successful and in May of 1641 Wentworth was beheaded. (Laud, and even King Charles himself, would soon follow him to the executioner's block.)

Massereene's story, however, had only just begun. Already, he had sown the seeds of two of the most momentous episodes in the histories of Britain and Ireland. His position and influence he had used to lead into the political arena the young Oliver Cromwell; to some in Ireland, Massereene himself might be seen as Cromwell's precursor for his 'speech delivered to the House of Commons that the conversion of the Papists in Ireland was only to be effected by the Bible in one hand and the sword in the other'. But as the English and Ulster-Scot nonconformists in Antrim celebrated the success of their Massereene champion, the Gaelic Irish were preparing a bloody rebellion for which Antrim would pay dearly.

THE 1641 REBELLION

If Lord Massereene's success in helping to rid Ireland of the accursed Earl of Strafford led Antrim's Protestants to anticipate some freedom of worship, the Gaelic Irish took it as their opportunity to wreak revenge upon the English intruder. Although it was initially intended to direct the rising against the English settlers rather than the Ulster-Scot, the furious resort to arms inevitably led to uncontrollable sectarian massacres and, consequently, retaliations.

On the eve of the rebellion, the fame of Sir John Clotworthy (who was championing Puritan rule of Ireland from his seat in the fiercely – Protestant House of Commons in London) was temporarily eclipsed at home by one of his lowly Irish servants at Antrim Castle – Owen O'Connolly.

'One of the rebel leaders, Major M'Mahon, believing that Owen O'Connolly would identify himself with the Irish conspiracy, disclosed to him the plans for surprising and taking Dublin Castle and destroying all the Protestants in the kingdom. O'Connolly was amazed at his friend's folly, hastened to the castle and told the story of the plot. Alarm was excited. The castle, though well stocked with arms and ammunition, had a force of only fifty men!

The gates were at once secured, watches were set at various points and strangers and suspicious persons were noted. One of the first steps taken was the arrest of Major M'Mahon, who admitted his guilt but declared that his death would not prevent a rising. Finding the officials on the alert, many engaged in the plot escaped. The timely warning, though it did not prevent the rebellion elsewhere, prevented in Dublin a dreadful massacre and a reign of anarchy,' wrote one of Clotworthy's officers in his report: *The Warr in Ireland, 1641–52.*

O'Connolly returned to Antrim Castle a national hero. Clotworthy, who had persuaded Parliament to station seven hundred infantry and a troop of cavalry at Antrim, appointed O'Connolly to captain a regiment. During Sir John's absence, his younger brother – James, of Moneymore – had gathered the Scottish and English settlers about Antrim into the castle and prepared for the worst.

Rebellion broke out late in 1641. Horrific massacres were recorded, particularly in Ulster. In January 1642, for example, Roman Catholics were massacred on Island Magee in retaliation for the murders of Protestants in Kilrea. One of Sir John Clotworthy's officers recalled:

"I remember about Christmas, there came to us at Antrim, with their Captain, one Lindsay, a civil man, who loved no murder, with about forty horsemen as a Troop, all formerly living at Tullahoge, who left their wives and children with their goods with the enemy, who all concluded they were all destroyed, and in revenge they could not endure to see any Irishman, but they must beat him to destroy him.

So one night they left Antrim, their garrison, unknown to all their officers but their own Lieutenant, Barnet Lindsay, and fell on Mr Upton's tenants, a gentleman who hated to see or hear innocent blood drawn, and would save them if he could, but was then in Carrickfergus; and they murdered about eighty persons, men, women and children, near Templepatrick."

On February 11, four thousand Irish rebels, led by Turlough O'Neill, surrounded Antrim. Two days later 'they made three parties of themselves,' according to an eye-witness; '(all the pikemen have a shafe or two of corn on his pike) with ten or twelve as fyle leaders and about forty or fifty deep in each fyle, which was an odd way to attack a town. They attacked at the Townhead Gate at the Flanker next to the Mill, and at Parker's Gate, being the gate as you go out of town to Shane's Castle. The party that charged the Townhead Gate and the Flanker came no nearer than a pike's length, who were so galled out of the Flanker, that they fell back and lost about fifteen killed. Those who advanced to the Mill Flanker did not much better, and those at Parker's Gate nothing at all, but retired'.[28]

The retreat was across the Sixmilewater and through Muckamore and Oldstone to the lough shore. Fields of crops were set ablaze as they fled.

Tradition holds that the Irish commandeered many of the country church buildings and, having fortified them, the English had to shell and burn the buildings to drive out their enemy. This would explain the 17th century cannon ball found amid coffined and unburied dead in the ancient Dundesart monastery, near the Crumlin River. Kilbride church and village were completely destroyed at this period. The *Dublin Penny Journal* (1833) contains a detailed description of a 48 ft by 15 ft church, attached to Antrim Round Tower, which was laid in ruins during the rebellion begun in 1641.

Fearing further attacks on Antrim, the following day Sir John Clotworthy went personally to Carrickfergus and secured an extra three hundred dragoons for Antrim Castle. With such reinforcements, Antrim survived repeated assaults by the rebels (though a typhus epidemic at the time was a different story). Parliament then provided the necessary finance for Clotworthy to expand his miniature fleet on Lough Neagh.

A few weeks later, a dozen large boats, each carrying sixty armed men, set sail from Antrim – an offensive against the rebels who had captured Charlemont and Mountjoy – behind the six brass guns aboard Clotworthy's 20-ton flagship, *The Sidney*.

However, they ran into one of the lough's freak storms which sank five of the fleet. Clotworthy made for the shelter of Ram's Island. Unknown to him, the island was thronged with rebels routed from the Antrim engagements! Luckily, a lull in the storm encouraged Clotworthy to turn about and return to Antrim instead of landing on the island.

Later, the Irish captured one of Clothworthy's boats 'in which were 2 brass cannon, 10 muskets, 12 barrels of salted fish, some sailors, and a company of soldiers. All were brought to Charlemont where some of the men were hanged and some redeemed'.[11] On another occasion, the Irish captured 7 more of the Antrim fleet and executed twenty soldiers.

It was Owen O'Connolly and Sir John's Muckamore relative, Captain Langford, who finally liberated the forts of Charlemont and Mountjoy from Irish occupation. Their 1643 naval battle with the Irish flotilla is among the most dramatic events in the history of Lough Neagh. At almost no cost to themselves, they killed sixty rebels and returned to Antrim in triumph with the captured flotilla and rebel prisoners.

A Scottish Covenanting Army, ten thousand strong, arrived to protect their fellow countrymen in Ulster from further attacks and to restore order. Initially, this was good news for the townsfolk of Antrim. Regimental chaplains helped the Presbyterians of Antrim, Templepatrick and Ballymena to be among the first congregations to organise their self-governments and elect elders. And to great rejoicing, Sir John Clotworthy brought to them (and Ireland) the Solemn League and Covenant.

But the officer commanding the thistle warriors was Major General Robert Monro. Though Oliver Cromwell would throw his old friend, Clotworthy, into prison and hand Antrim Castle to the turncoat, Owen O'Connolly, it would be Monro who would wipe Antrim from the face of the map.

THE BURNING OF ANTRIM

Oliver Cromwell had the first Lord Massereene (Sir John Clotworthy) to thank for his initial 'break' in politics. Sir John had used his influence to help Cromwell take the first step on the road to political power.

Their friendship was one casualty when the Long Parliament split in two. As a conservative Presbyterian loyal to King Charles 1, Clotworthy found himself opposed by Cromwell's radical Independents. When Clotworthy protested at the arrest of the monarch, Cromwell had him impeached by the House of Commons.

With charges of high treason pending, Sir John and six fellow-Presbyterian members of the House slipped out of London and made for the Kent coast. Cromwellian soldiers caught up with them in the middle of the English Channel, as Cobett's *State Trials* record:–

> "Within six miles of Calais, seeing themselves pursued, made hard to windward to escape, but could not: Captain Lamming plying them hard with small shot, and a frigate man of war coming in to the assistance, the Six Members pulled down sail and yielded."

Clotworthy escaped, however, and found refuge in France. Five months later he was allowed to return to Parliament. Shortly afterwards, though, he was one of the Members violently thrown out of the Commons. His opposition to the trial and execution of Charles cost him three years imprisonment 'first at an inn in the Strand, and subsequently at the Gatehouse in Westminster'.

Meanwhile, Cromwell decided that Royalists in Ireland, opposed to his new republic, needed crushing, and Protestant deaths in the 1641 Rebellion needed avenging. Consequently, Cromwell arrived in Ireland and, through a massacre at Drogheda, opened the gateway to Ulster.

Former servant boy at Antrim Castle, Owen O'Connolly (whom Clotworthy had made a regimental captain) welcomed Cromwellian soldiers to Antrim in 1648. O'Connolly swore allegiance to the Cromwellian Independents and was rewarded with promotion to commader-in-chief of the Antrim garrison.

News soon reached O'Connolly that Major General Robert Monro and his Covenanting army planned to attack Antrim Castle. O'Connolly sped to Belfast where he secured about a hundred cavalry to reinforce the Antrim garrison. On the road home, however, at Dunadry, he encountered some 140 cavalry and 800 infantry; Monro forces under the command of Colonel John Hamilton. O'Connolly lost twenty men and was himself seriously wounded 'and carried with no more respect than a dead ox behind a man to Connor, where he immediately died'. The following day, O'Connolly's remains were retrieved from Connor and interred in Antrim's parish churchyard. The royalist army pressed on to Antrim. One of their officers has left us this account of what took place (in 1649):

> "A combined Royalist and Irish force came before Antrim and summoned the town to yield to the King. But those within the Castle, one of Cromwell's captains with his company and one Lieut. Devlin with a Troop, returned answer that they would not yield the Castle; on which the town was assaulted and burned, and some were commanded to fire at The Mount and Castle, but to little purpose. Being a place not fit for a running party to attack."

Though the castle did not fall to Monro, the town did. He razed Antrim to the ground. The parish church too suffered considerable fire damage. It was to take more than seventy years to properly rebuild the town. The official history of the church states that it was not rebuilt until 1720 yet there are records of various independent ministers officiating in it during Commonwealth times.

A dozen of Antrim Castle's defenders died in the attack, but the castle itself remained firmly in Cromwellian hands. With Monro forced to march away and Lord Massereene languishing in a Cromwellian jail, the people of Antrim must have wondered where the story of Antrim would go from here.

RESTORATION

In 1660, Sir John Clotworthy was chosen by England's Parliament to invite the Prince Charles to accept the English throne. Ireland's 'General Convention' Parliament also invited Sir John 'to proceed to Holland to wait upon Charles, and induce him to comply with certain specified conditions applicable to Ireland'; and though he was prevented from reaching the Prince, the election of him for such a purpose shows that he possessed a large measure of public confidence.

On behalf of the Irish people, it was Sir John Clotworthy who welcomed King Charles 2 to London.

With the Monarchy restored, Sir John at once complained that he had been deprived of his royal pension by the 'late unlawful power' of the Commonwealth; as compensation, Cromwell had given Clotworthy a 99-years lease of Lough Neagh:

> "With the fishing and soil thereof and the islands therein called Ram's Island and Coney Island containing three acres of ground, also the Lough and river of Bann as far as the Salmon Leap, containing six salmon fishings and two mixed fishings of salmon and eels, and another of trouts."

King Charles not only ratified Cromwell's grant, but also made Sir John Clotworthy one of his first and closest of Privy Councillors and raised him to the Peerage with the title First Viscount Massereene and Baron of Lough Neagh. A further appointment made Lord Massereene the Governor of Londonderry.

Homesick for Antrim, the new Lord Massereene returned to the valley of the Sixmilewater. Many troubled years had passed since he had fled his father's old Antrim artillery-keep 'castle', and three years more passed before Sir John had completed the stately new Castle of Antrim (later modified and developed by succeeding Massereenes):

> "It was quadrangular, of three stories, embellished and strengthened by four square towers, one at each angle. The windows in the rear looked into a small yard in the centre. The walls were of great strength, six feet in depth. The roof of the northern wing, which presents a side front to the river terrace, had six pointed gables, in the style of the old French chateau, and terminated at the northern end in a plain turretted gable. Half-a-dozen granite steps led from the ground level to the grand entrance door, which opened into the hall from a small stone platform, protected by a stone trellice. The hall itself, square and spacious, had in it one of the large old-fashioned fireplaces, capable of holding an entire kish of turf, with its complement of bog fir. To the left a breakfast and dining parlour. At the back the staircase led to the sleeping apartments. To the right was the 'buttery', since transformed into a study and housekeeper's room. In the wall of the buttery, at an elevation of three feet from the floor, a small square door, through which food was handed to the poor as they entered the hall, for that was the custom in the good olden times. The castle was protected on the west by the river, which washed its wall on that side, whilst the three other sides – north, east, and south – were guarded by a broad and deep moat communicating with the river, whence it was kept constantly filled with water. To the north and south were two bastions; the southern commanded the town, and the northern the lake. The entire – bawn, and bastions, moat, castle and courtyard – was enclosed within five acres, three rods and one perch."[52]
> (Charles Henry O'Neill, 1860)

Along the lough shore, a thousand acres were added to the estate by the Crown, for use as a deer park (1665).

More than half a century of reconstruction lay ahead for Antrim town: two decades of war had left their mark.

The most common surnames found in Antrim at this time were Adire, Armstrong, Blair, Boyd, Browne, Crawford, Donnell, Farguson, Graham, Hunter, Johnson, Kenedy, Loggan, Millar, Montgomery, Moore, McAlester, McIlroy, McKinstry, McKye, O'Hara, O'Heveran, O'Neill, Read, Russell, Taggart and Wallace.

The three or four hundred townspeople of 1665 learned from their aristocratic lord that if they possessed 'the convenience for boiling a pot', they had now the privilege of returning two members to the Irish Parliament in Dublin; Antrim had become a 'potwalloping borough'. In practice, of course, such Members 'ought' to be Massereenes and the appointments would further advance the personal fortunes of that illustrious family. Antrim accordingly obliged by 'selecting' Sir John and his son-in-law, Sir John Skeffington of Fisherwick, Staffordshire.

The principal event of Lord Massereene's final years involved a secret plot by Presbyterians to overthrow the power of the bishops of the Established Church. In Antrim (and Down), however, Presbyterians refused to have anything to do with the plot to take control of Dublin Castle by force. Information from an informer led to the arrests of the main conspirators as they attempted to storm the castle; one was placed under house-arrest at Massereene's Dublin residence. Every Presbyterian minister found in Antrim and Down was apprehended and imprisoned at Carrickfergus. The leaders of the plot were sentenced to death. One was 'tempted by some then about Court to accuse Lord Massereene of the plot, they being jealous of Lord Massereene at that time, in exchange for pardon;' he refused, and was executed.

Massereene's political opponents may have taken some comfort a little later when ill health forced his lordship to return to the seclusion of Antrim Castle. Shortly afterwards, the spectacular career of the old Elizabethan adventurer's son came to a close. In death, Sir John Clotworthy, 1st Lord Massereene, was accorded a grand funeral to Saint Patrick's Cathedral, Dublin, where he lies buried. (His wife and daughter are buried in All Saints' Parish Church, Antrim.)

1665–1690

Before the days of King Charles 2, the first Lord Massereene had lost Antrim Castle to the Cromwellians. After Charles' reign, the second Lord Massereene abandoned the castle to the Irish Jacobites.

The Hon. Mary Clotworthy, being the only child and heir of Sir John Clotworthy, became mistress of Antrim Castle on her father's death in 1665. Her husband, who succeeded to the title – 2nd Viscount Massereene – was Sir John Skeffington of Fisherwick, Staffordshire.

The De Skeffyngtons were of ancient Norman extraction and had risen to power under Henry 8. Henry had appointed Sir William Skeffington, in 1529, as H.M. Commissioner to Ireland. Sir William's great-great-grandson had been created a baronet by Charles 1, and it was this baronet's grandson who became 2nd Viscount Massereene in default of male issue of the 1st Viscount. The family seat was Skeffyngton Hall, beside the field of Naseby where Cromwell's victory over Charles 1 decided the Civil War. (The whole district is still one of elegant mansions, such as the former home at Althorp of the present Princess of Wales.)

When Sir John accompanied his wife home to Antrim he found himself lord of some 45,000 Massereene acres from Dunluce to Tipperary. At first, they enjoyed the good life in Antrim. From one of the oak trees in his Antrim Castle Grounds, Sir John leisurely carved himself a grand armchair; this he placed on top of the (old motte) 'Mount' (or 'Mound'), from where, on summer days, he loved to supervise the rebuilding of the town which had suffered so much at the hands of the Irish, Scot Covenanters and Cromwellians. Though Member of the Irish Parliament for the county of Antrim, he preferred the domestic bliss of Antrim Castle to the public frenzy of Dublin Castle.

In 1671 Lord Massereene invited a celebrated English Puritan theologian to become the resident chaplain at Antrim Castle. John Howe had once been private chaplain to Oliver Cromwell and, later, performed the same office for Cromwell's son, Richard. After the Restoration, Howe refused to subscribe to the Act of Uniformity and, as a dissenter, 'having been chased out of England on theological grounds took refuge with our people and preached with freedom in the parish church for some years'.[28]

Howe conducted services in the parish church every Sunday afternoon during the five years he lived at the castle. There he wrote two great Christian classics – *The Vanity of this Mortal Life* and *The Good Man, the Living Temple of God* – for which books he still earns a place in both Webster's and Chambers' modern biographical dictionaries. Said one historian:

> "We picture him to ourselves wandering along the shores of Lough Neagh, and through the bosky woods from which one of the mysterious round towers still rises above the trees, as when he lived close by. While here he sat with the Presbytery, and regularly preached weekly in the parish church by special favour. One of his best books, that on 'Delighting in God' was published during his residence at Antrim. With the sanction of the Presbyterian Church he also taught in what may be called the Presbyterian College of the period. For, in conjunction with the Rev. Thomas Gowan, minister of Antrim, he instructed students at that place in theology and philosophy – doubtless a most valuable service at a time when there was no other means in Ireland of training candidates for the Presbyterian ministry than such a 'school of philosophy'."[78]

Andre Le Nôtre (Louis XIV's designer of the Versailles Palace Gardens), is reputed to have landscaped the Castle Grounds at Antrim as a unique mini-Versailles for the 2nd Viscount Massereene; the author, however, has been unable to find documentary proof.

The quiet peace of Antrim was abruptly shattered when James 2 succeeded Charles 2. James' Patriot Parliament in Dublin rejected Westminster's authority and decided to annex Protestant holdings in Ireland, such as Antrim Castle.

The Jacobites jailed William King, D.D. for furnishing treasonable information to the Duke of Schomberg. King, afterwards Archbishop of Dublin, was born (1650) in Antrim, the son of a lowly Scots miller who had migrated to Antrim between 1639–49 to escape the Solemn League and Covenant. It was the recently-retired vicar of Antrim, Canon Thornton, (who studiously examined King's personal papers at Trinity College, Dublin) who first drew the present author's attention to King – perhaps the most intriguing of all Antrim's sons of yore. W. S. Smith offers a useful though brief glimpse of King's career in his *Historical Gleanings*. The historian, Macaulay, drew a fine pen-portrait of King in just one sentence: 'It was only after he had been repeatedly imprisoned by the Government, to which he was devotedly attached; after he had been insulted and threatened in his choir by soldiers; after he had been interdicted from burying in his own church-yard; from preaching in his own pulpit; after he had narrowly escaped with his life from a musket-shot fired at him in the streets, that he began to think the Whig theory of government less unreasonable and unchristian than it had once appeared to him.'

When Lord Massereene learned that James 2's Irish Jacobite army was marching towards Antrim he quickly packed his bags and fled with his wife to catch the Derry boat to England.

With the garrison of Belfast routed, the Jacobites of Lieutenant General Hamilton were on the march to Coleraine, via Antrim. The garrison at Antrim Castle followed their lordship's example and promptly deserted their posts. Hamilton, finding the gates of Antrim and its castle lying open and the place deserted, took possession not only of the castle but also 'Lord Massereene's plate, and other valuable property, which were pointed out where concealed by one of his own servants – not leaving him so much as a silver spoon'. The loss of property was later estimated at around three thousand pounds.

Loyal Protestants in Antrim, however, took some comfort from a widely-known report that:

> "In the reign of Charles 2, in the year 1650, at a season of great difficulty and tribulation among the people, a Synod of the Presbyterian clergy was held at Antrim, and among the members in attendance one aged minister sat apparently drowsy whilst the others were earnestly engaged in some passing debate. The minister, on being asked if he were taking a nap, replied: 'No; my soul has been ravished with a glorious vision of the happy days which the Church of God, in these kingdoms, shall enjoy under a Prince of Orange!'"[7]

About this tale, a Ballymena newspaper noted (in 1857): 'The fact of this occurrence was related, attested, and placed on record previous to the death of Charles 2, and, of course, long before King William claimed the Crown or had any connection whatever with the affairs of Britain.' The minister was plainly out of the same mould as Patrick and his fantastically-prophetic successors!

When the Apprentice Boys of Derry slammed shut those famous city gates, Lord Massereene's son, young Colonel Clotworthy Skeffington, found himself and his Antrim militia locked out and facing the approach of King James and his Jacobite army! Skeffington – 'a man of energy and courage, and possessed of considerable military knowledge for a country gentleman' – shot at the sentry on the city's walls and threatened to burn down the gates. He and his men were then quickly admitted and there they stayed until the Mountjoy arrived to relieve the famous siege.

The Prince of Orange put paid to James' grand ambitions on 1st July (old calendar), 1690, at the river Boyne. With the coronation of William 3, old Viscount Massereene was able to return home to Antrim and take his House of Peers seat in the new Williamite parliament in Dublin.

Colonel Clotworthy Skeffington, who had married a Somerset girl (Rachael Hungerford), married off his daughter Rachael to Randall, 4th Earl of Antrim, and succeeded to the title of 3rd Viscount Massereene when his father was laid to rest (1695) in Antrim Parish Churchyard.

But finally, as the 17th century curtain drops, spare a thought for the unfortunate young Antrim lady who, in 1698, vomited horse-dung, needles, pins, hair, feathers, pieces of thread and glass, nails of various sorts, an iron knife, eggs and the remains of shell-fish! Beats the 'old lady who swallowed a fly'. I don't know why the old lady swallowed the fly but the Antrim lassie, history records, was bewitched! The latter eventually recovered (from the effects of her obviously unhealthy appetite), but the 'witch' was tried, hung and finally burned. 'I imagine, if any inhabitant of Antrim of the present day swallowed what would start in a small way a marine store in business, as this girl appears to have done, that inhabitant would be equally "bewitched" with the young lady of (three) centuries ago.'[28]

THE EIGHTEENTH CENTURY

It came in like a lamb but it was not long before the new century showed signs of going out like a lion, if community tensions had not exploded before then.

In the early years, the drama for Antrim town was primarily architectural. Though still towerless and spireless, the parish church acquired its handsome gateposts, (inscribed with the vicar's name – Rev. J. Finiston), and the churchyard's perimeter wall which would later – see 'Battle of Antrim' pp. 41-46 – be the bane of the Massereenes and, much later, more of a bane to vehicular traffic. All this, however, would have been little in comparison with the spectacle of a new, stone-built meeting-house which the Scots-Presbyterians had erected in Scotch Quarter (Church Street), to usher in the new century.

When the Episcopalians, in 1673, charged the Presbyterians (who only had the parish church as a place for their worship), not to 'profane the Sabbath by attending at the (parish) church door while it (the Liturgy) is reading', the hint was taken.

Old Presbyterian Meeting House (before restoration 1891–92) – Courtesy of Ulster Museum.

Sometime during the next ten years, the Presbyterians moved to an old, thatched barn – 'The Little House' – at Meeting-House Field (near the Steeple).

Just sixteen years later, however, a lease – dated June 9, 1699 – was acquired for the Scotch Quarter site of their First (Old) Antrim Presbyterian Meeting-House. Its minister in 1888 fondly recalled – 'its whitewashed exterior, its cruciform form, its outer gallery stairs, its small, irregularly-placed leaded windows, its heavy creaking doors, with old-fashioned latches, its broad aisles, and still more roughly-hewn supports, its old clock in the gallery front that ticked its last tick generations since, and the high pulpit with its massive sounding-board . . .'[28] The present writer does not think that the old building – today's headquarters of Antrim Boxing Club – was originally cruciform, notwithstanding that the above minister knew the old Meeting House for almost a decade before it was rebuilt in 1881. Originally, the building appears to have been of conventional Reformation design: no altar and the pulpit taken half-way down one wall with the pews turned to face it. Later, galleries were fitted at each end. But from the 1720s onwards, often a wing was added opposite the pulpit to form a T-shape if a congregation grew too big; this form of Tau cross is this meeting-house's shape in the 1833 and 1859 O.S. maps.

The young minister, John Abernethy (1680–1740), appointed to this congregation in 1703, was the son of Moneymore's famous Rev. John Abernethy. The latter was in England, delivering an address of congratulations in 1689 to Prince William of Orange, when his children were evacuated to Derry, where they perished during the historic siege of that city. Young John, however, survived (because he had been visiting relations at Ballymena).

During his early days in Antrim he was alarmed to find Calvinism sweeping through Ulster Presbyterian churches. Ulster pulpits were being crowded with Scottish preachers who had signed (or 'subscribed') their names as a token of belief in Cornelius Burges' 1646 *Confession of Faith,* (which, during the Protectorate, had superseded the Thirty-nine Articles as the authoritative doctrine of the Church of England. The Confession was sanctioned by the Westminster Assembly of Divines, which body had been attended by Sir John Clotworthy as a lay assessor).

It was at The Belfast Society – of which he was the founder (and a leading spirit, along with Revs. Wm. Taylor of Randalstown and Alexander Brown of Donegore) – where, in 1719 our John Abernethy preached a famous sermon declaring his opposition to the Church's attempt to make 'subscription' compulsory: he denied that the Church had any right to make people subscribe to statements of belief; 'there should be no creed other than the Bible'. For preaching this sermon, Abernethy was accused of attempting to give 'New Light' to the world, and from this time the Non-Subscribers were known as the 'New Light people'.

As a result, Abernethy's First (Old) Antrim and sixteen sympathetic congregations were officially excluded from the Synod of Ulster Presbyterians and formed into the (new) Non-Subscribing Presbytery of Antrim (1725).

John Abernethy ministered in Antrim for twenty seven years before answering a call from Wood Green congregation, Dublin. His grandson, Dr John Abernethy (b. 1764, London), for his surgical skills and humorous sayings, attracted large crowds to his lectures in St Bartholomew's Hospital, London.

An effective counteractive to the 'New Light' – Secederism – was first planted in Ireland by the people of Lylehill. Seemingly, events began with the expiration of a Rickamore farm's lease, whereupon the landlord, Col. Upton (an elder in the Templepatrick Pres. Ch.) awarded it to Rev. Wm. Livingstone (or his son), minister of Templepatrick. Lylehill members of Livingstone's congregation promptly withdrew, applied to be taken under the care of the Associate Presbytery in Scotland and, in 1746, were supplied with Rev. Isaac Patton, a licentiate of the Assoc. Presbytery of Dunfermline. 'A humble church was soon erected for the accommodation of the people, and so, within sixteen miles,' if the crow flies straight, 'from the spot where Edward Brice, in 1613, planted the standard of Presbyterianism, originated the cause of the Secession in Ireland – a cause which was to exercise so useful an influence in the province during a separate existence of a hundred years, and finally to merge its life, along with the Synod of Ulster, in the united General Assembly of the Presbyterian Church.'[78]

Abernethy's non-subscribers, a hundred years on, became known as Unitarians. At that time, the remonstrances of Rev. Dr Henry Montgomery (b. 1788, fifth son of Archibald Montgomery of Boltnaconnell House, Killead) – one of the greatest orators Ulster has ever produced – rekindled the old spirit of independence and helped ensure the survival of The Presbytery of Antrim to the present day. ('Unitarian' was the popular name, rather in the way that the Society of Friends is popularly called the Quakers. John Abernethy and his friends would have been horrified at being called Unitarians as such maintain against the doctrine of the Trinity that God is one person.) In 1981, The Presbytery of Antrim presented Abernethy's old meeting-house and graveyard to the Borough Council of Antrim; its congregation has since joined the Old (Non-Subscribing) Congregation of Templepatrick.

Another dramatic consequence of Abernethy's famous sermon was that ninety of the families of his Antrim congregation saw fit to withdraw and form (1726) a new and subscribing congregation, attached to The Templepatrick Presbytery.

Curiously, The Templepatrick Presbytery also had a Rev. John Abernethy (1736–1818), a son of Templepatrick village's Josias Abernethy:–

"He was a bright and luminous preacher,
A sound and honest moral teacher;
A subtle, abstract metaphysician,
A shrewd and able politician.
He knew the system of creation
Better than most men of the nation;
And sat sedately at his ease,
And ate his butter, bread and cheese."

Mill Row Meeting House.

He retired to Antrim after being removed from the ministry for 'celebrating irregular marriages'.

Antrim's new Subscribers – whose third minister, Rev. A. Montgomery, would be suspended from ministerial duty for 'celebrating marriages in an irregular manner' – lodged for a spell in 'office houses' at Antrim Castle. Finally, in 1731, they erected a new meeting-house at Mill Row (Riverside). It was this congregation which would become the First Antrim Presbyterians we recognise today.

1726 also marked the erection of what is today one of the richest classical (Florentine style) buildings in Ireland and the oldest courthouse in the Province: Antrim Market and Court House. Sir Clotworthy Skeffington, 4th Viscount (1713–38) – whose father had already provided the folk of Massereene district with the 1708 stone Massereene Bridge access to Antrim – had received £150 from the Grand Jury of the county 'towards building and carrying on a Session House in the town of Antrim in and for said county'. It came too late for the notorious highwayman, Eneas 'Nessie' O'Haughan, who, before he was hung in 1724, buried his topboot – brimming with gold sovereigns – on the western slope of McIlwan's Hill at Ballyutoag, near the Clady end of the 'Seven Mile Straight' – or so they say. The story has not yet been proved right, (or wrong)!

Notwithstanding the severity and, indeed, the barbarity of the criminal laws – transportation or death for comparatively trivial offences – the Courthouse was to witness many cases of highway robbery and thefts of cattle, sheep, horses, and of linen from bleach greens.

Access to the courtroom on the first floor of the Market House (where petty sessions are still conducted), was afforded by the grand flight of double steps at the west end. Below, between rows of imposing pillars, the ground floor served as a market hall. It served as a focal point in the Market Square where, since 1665, the Massereenes had made use of their patent to hold fairs on the first days of May, July and October and the fourth days of June, August and November. Massereene had introduced long-horned English cattle to improve local breeding; his year-old bulls each sold for £5!

And the Huguenots, whom King William 3 had encouraged to settle in Ulster, were developing the local linen industry. The Scots spinners and weavers in Antrim's thatched Scotch Quarter found their market opening up as demand increased across Europe and as far away as the West Indies, though most of the linen produced went to Britain.

William 3's court printer – Daniel Blow – founded a paper-manufacturing mill at Dunadry which continued production throughout the century.

The Anglo-Irish link strengthened with Britain exercising control over the Irish Parliament. The Protestant Ascendancy was secured now by a Dublin parliament of landed gentry – Massereene was an Irish peer for the Borough of Antrim – and the Established (Episcopal) Church.

Roman Catholic Irish were denied any religious or political freedom, many emigrating to enlist in European armies. Dissenting Protestants too had religious and civic grievances which would contribute towards catapulting the Ulster-Scots into the headlines of Irish and, indeed, world history.

NINE ANTRIMS

The United States town of Suffern, in New York State, owes its foundation to the story of Antrim. Its founder, John Suffern, settled there in the 18th century, and christened his new settlement 'New Antrim' after his North of Ireland home town. Nine new Antrims were created in North America during the 1700s by emigrants from our town.

Life in old Antrim a couple of centuries ago was rough for men like John Suffern and David Waugh. Being the sons of Scottish 'planters', they were Presbyterians. In Antrim – as in many another Ulster town – the 18th century was unkind to such sturdy-minded people whose spirit of independence was to write stirring chapters in the history of Ulster and North America before the century was out.

Six bad harvests at the start of the century began the exodus of Antrim (and Ulster) Scots to the North American colonies. Then recessions in the linen industry and rocketing prices combined with further bad harvests (making it difficult for Antrim's Presbyterian small-farmers to pay the rent). Arthur Young complained that the rundale system operating about Antrim could make these small farmers destitute if for example, just one cow died![31] Thousands were now journeying to the ports of Portrush and Belfast to seek a new beginning in the New World.

Episcopalian Archbishop Boulter, alarmed at the growing numbers of thrifty, hard-working 'Scotch-Irish' abandoning towns like Antrim, protested to the Secretary of State:

> The whole north is in ferment, and every day people are engaging one another to go next year. The humour has spread like a contagious distemper, and the people will hardly hear anyone who tries to cure them of their madness.

The landed gentry, however, were not listening to Boulter. At Shane's Castle, for example, there was the preoccupation of assembling hundreds of local men, armed with seven pieces of cannon, to repel the ex-Glenarm general who had led (1760) a successful invasion of Carrickfergus and Belfast by French troops; unique in being the only French victory on British soil (since 1066).

There was no landed gent at Antrim Castle, however: Sir Clotworthy Skeffington, 5th Viscount and 1st Earl of Massereene, had 'paused (1757) at the ruins of the old Abbey of Massereene, when suddenly uttering a loud cry and the name of one long dead he fell down and expired while his dogs moaned round him in a piteous manner';[52] his heir was not yet come of age.

At Castle Upton, however, Clotworthy Upton was heightening agrarian discontent among his Presbyterian small-farmer tenants by pushing up farm rents to exhorbitant levels; ninety three of his farms were offered for letting in just one advertisement of the *Belfast News Letter* on 12 May, 1767. (The land-leases granted by William 3 had expired in 1770.) Astronomical rent increases evicted thousands of Presbyterians from Lord Donegall's Antrim estates. Homeless, and bitter that their 1690 contribution to British freedom should be so soon forgotten, many of the Ulster-Scots now followed their former kinsmen, along the 'flax route', to the young colonies across the wild North Atlantic.

Against the sea of troubles at home, many took up arms in the secret 'Hearts of Steel' society, proclaiming:

> ". . . betwixt landlord and rectors, the very marrow is screwed out of our bones, and our lives are even become so burdensome to us, by these uncharitable and unreasonable men, that we do not care whether we live or die; for they lay such burthen upon our shoulders that they cannot touch them with one of their fingers; they have reduced us to such a deplorable state by such grievous oppressions that the poor is turned black in the face, and the skin parched on their back."
>
> Hearts of Steel Proclamation, March 1772.

1,200 Templepatrick Steelmen, wielding crowbars, marched on Belfast to demand the release of one of their imprisoned members. Had their demand not been met, it is likely that the whole of the city would have burned to the ground. Nowhere were the agrarian crimes of the Steelmen more violent than about Antrim. Nonetheless, within three years they too had transported their anti-British resentments to American soil.

Antrim's exiles became celebrated frontiersmen in the new America. The David Waughs, who acquired vast plantations, erected fortified farmsteads for new settlers. They built meeting-houses too, along with 'little red school-houses', and called the lot – New Antrims. Some still flourish today, and the author extends greetings from Old Antrim. The Ulster-Scot, or 'Scotch-Irish' way of life here and in the New World is graphically portrayed in Omagh's Ulster-American Folk Park. From County Antrim alone emigrated forefathers of U.S.A. Presidents Nos. 7, 17, 21, 23, 24, 25, 26 and 28!

How the Scotch-Irish played a critically decisive role in declaring, winning and strengthening independence for the United States of America is a gripping tale, unfortunately outside the parameters of *The Story of Antrim*.

The American War of Independence prevented any further emigration for much of the rest of the century. If the people of Antrim had any grievances – and both Presbyterians and Roman Catholics here had plenty – they would have to be resolved at home. The disaffected were bent on breaking the political power of the governing class by challenging them at the ballot box. But the aristocratic Massereenes considered their traditional representation of the borough in the Irish Parliament a sinecure which no-one was going to take away from them. (See 'The People versus The Aristocrats', p. 35).

THE HOUNDS OF ANTRIM

A dog died in Dublin in the last year of the 18th century, and thereby hangs a tale.

His master was that extraordinary eccentric 9th Baronet, 6th Viscount and 2nd Earl of Massereene, Clotworthy Skeffington. (His bizarre capers, which would make a stirring chapter for this present book, have already been vividly chronicled by Dr A. P. W. Malcolmson in his aptly named book: *The Extraordinary Career of the 2nd Earl of Massereene, 1743–1805*.[50] Be it sufficient here to whet your appetite.)

Clotworthy twice served long prison sentences, and was thrice married – the first two times to the same girl, who, for his love, twice organised jailbreaks for him and was, herself, twice imprisoned as a consequence.

And then was deserted when he sought the affections of a bawdy London chambermaid. She became mistress not only of her lord but of all that he surveyed in Ireland which included the ancestral family seat and estate in Antrim and imposing family mansion in Dublin.

He led her a dog's life, but his dog led hers, for that four-legged beast seems ever to have been his first love; for, as the proverb says – unlike women, 'a dog doesn't bark at its master'!

When the animal died, at Clotworthy's Dublin residence, it first lay in state on the drawing-room carpet, but her ladyship's bed lay in a state when it was used later for two wakes.

> Now this tale I tell, it is no joke –
> They waked it twice but the dog never woke;
> And of the three sad figures about that bed,
> The most unfortunate – being dead –
> Was nor either the lord, nor his dame,
> But dog Rufus, departed, if that was his name.
> If no fun you find in my verse, well –
> Enjoy the pun and call it doggerel.

Perhaps Samuel Taylor Coleridge (who could write verse), could also have been thinking of this affair when, just before the dog's death he wrote:

> "Thy lap-dog, Rufus, is a dainty beast.
> It don't surprise me in the least
> To see thee lick so dainty a beast.
> But that so dainty-clean a beast licks thee –
> Yes – that surprises me."

Clotworthy's canine may have been born a dog but it died a gentleman. When the grand funeral procession arrived from Dublin, Antrim dogs were compelled to wear a black scarf and respectfully attend the burial service!

A century later an altogether less hilarious doggy funeral took place in the Castle Grounds. Beside the terrace gardens' glasshouses, the Viscountess laid to rest her little pet dog, Jumbo, and erected above the spot an elaborate marble tablet, upon which these words were cut:

HERE LIES
JUMBO
THE MOST FAITHFUL AND DEVOTED
LITTLE DOG
(A VERY HANDSOME SMALL FOX TERRIER)
OF
VISCOUNT MASSEREENE
AND
FERRARD

WHO ERECTS THIS AS A TRIBUTE
TO HIS MEMORY AND OF HER
AFFECTION AND REGRET FOR HER
PET AND CONSTANT COMPANION
FOR FOURTEEN YEARS
DIED AT ANTRIM CASTLE
25th MARCH, 1896, AGED FOURTEEN YEARS

It's enough to bring the memory flooding back of that first adventurous Elizabethan Clotworthy who had the stone statue carved of his lady's hound and placed on the walls of Antrim Castle; proclaiming that as long as it remained there the Clotworthy family would endure.

Which, indeed, was very true, for, as Victor Hugo would remind us 'history has its truth, and so has legend hers'. (For official restoration), some present-day clot removed the Antrim statue, with a chisel, leaving only a stump of the tail. And thereby hangs a tale indeed, for fire has removed the Clotworthys' castle at Antrim, leaving only a stump of it; and, sadly, the Clotworthys have removed themselves, to England. (A new site – at Antrim Forum – has been found for the statue).

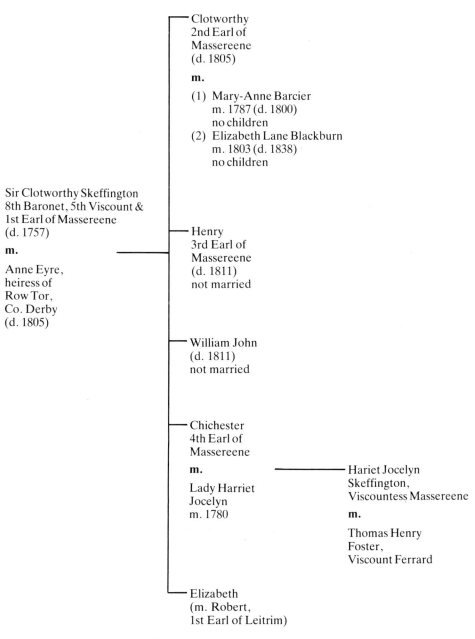

Clotworthy
2nd Earl of
Massereene
(d. 1805)

m.

(1) Mary-Anne Barcier
m. 1787 (d. 1800)
no children
(2) Elizabeth Lane Blackburn
m. 1803 (d. 1838)
no children

Sir Clotworthy Skeffington
8th Baronet, 5th Viscount &
1st Earl of Massereene
(d. 1757)

m.

Anne Eyre,
heiress of
Row Tor,
Co. Derby
(d. 1805)

Henry
3rd Earl of
Massereene
(d. 1811)
not married

William John
(d. 1811)
not married

Chichester
4th Earl of
Massereene

m.

Lady Harriet
Jocelyn
m. 1780

Hariet Jocelyn
Skeffington,
Viscountess Massereene

m.

Thomas Henry
Foster,
Viscount Ferrard

Elizabeth
(m. Robert,
1st Earl of Leitrim)

The Earls of Massereene

THE PEOPLE VERSUS THE ARISTOCRATS

While the 2nd Earl drifted about Europe, incurring debts amounting to £30,000 and spending eighteen years in prison (and would have served longer had not the Parisian mob liberated him during the French Revolution), his stepmother, the Dowager Countess Elizabeth Eyre (second wife of the 1st Earl) managed the Massereene estate.

Even if the antics of the 2nd Earl had not been bringing into greater and greater

Greenmount.

disrepute the name of Massereene, the Antrim weavers and spinners who congregated about The Massereene Arms hotel (established 1754), offered their loyalty, more and more, to the big house at the opposite end of the town from the castle – the Thompson mansion at Greenmount.

The Thompsons were Presbyterian Scots farmers who came to Antrim in the mid-17th century. In those times the family enjoyed a cordial relationship with the Massereenes: one Thompson was to be christened Skeffington and had a Massereene Skeffington as godfather. By the mid-18th century, Thompson fortunes had greatly increased: their two bleach greens at Greenmount were so profitable, Robert Thompson was able to rebuild (1820) his grand manor house at Greenmount, on an estate of two hundred acres (which, being in the Tirgracey townland, was not leased from the Massereenes). The Thompsons could also feel independent for other reasons: on land which they acquired at Ravensdale in Louth (and Meath), they had established a flourishing drapery business. They also possessed a £10,000 estate on the isle of St Kitts in the British West Indies, and a sugar plantation on the Danish West Indies isle of St Croix.

With their weaving of linen, calico and hosiery being marketed at the cloth fairs of Antrim, Oldstone, Shane's Castle, Randalstown and Ballymena, these Greenmount draper-landlords constituted a novel power to attract the political allegiance of sober, work-a-day Presbyterian tenants, farmers, clergy and laity radically opposed to both aristocratic influence and the power of the Established Church.

The Massereenes, observed Arthur Young, 'are very industrious but are much inclined to enjoy part of the effects of their industry in the society of their acquaintances and friends'.[31]

Antrim folk, invited to dinner at the Thompsons' table, felt themselves as privileged as their aristocratic contemporary the Duke of Marlborough who, when advising his wife about the necessity for an icehouse at Blenheim Palace, wrote: 'The hot weather makes me think . . . the most agreeable of all presents is that of summer ice'. Meals and drinks at Greenmount were complemented with the rare delicacy of 'summer ice'; the Thompsons had what the Massereenes (seemingly) had not – an ice house (which still exists at Greenmount in a fine state of preservation).

During the harsh winters which had contributed to so many of their kinsmen emigrating, Thompson farmhands carted blocks of ice from the estate pond to a circular, stone-built structure which was covered with an earth mound. An old account explains how the farm-hand: 'after laying down the ice outside the door, pounds it into particles not larger than those of sand or salt. He then carries it into the icehouse, and throws it into the ice well, in which a man is placed with a rammer to beat and ram closely, occasionally sprinkling with a little water to consolidate the whole. When this water is impregnated with salt at the rate of 10 lb. to 10 gallons and poured on the ice in such quantities as to saturate it completely, the ice will become as firm as rock, and will keep three times as long as when common water is used. It will also be found to keep much longer when exposed to the air. The reason is to be found in the well-known chemical fact, that salt water, and consequently salted ice, has a less capacity for heat than fresh water or fresh ice'.

The icehouse was primarily a refrigerated storehouse for the provision of 'summer ice' at the dinner table. (Food was preserved by drying, salting and pickling and stored in the manor house's cellars.) This winter-house, then, even in the height of summer, was always preserved, as we say – 'as cold as an ice-house'.

After dinner, the temperature rose as Thompson guests drank deep of their host's expressed ambition of wresting political control of Antrim from the church in the town centre and the castle at the town foot. If he could succeed there might be a brighter future for such infants of the day as William Orr and Henry Joy McCracken.

Discontent in the winter of 1769 was insufficient, nonetheless, for the Thompson Independents to overturn the Massereene's traditional vote. But within three months, Thomas Thompson unexpectedly found himself legal director of the Masereene estates and fortune!

The 2nd Earl, in need of some £12,000 expenses, had appointed a Cpt. John Clarke to procure capital by taking over the Dowager's control of Antrim. As a stranger to Antrim, Clarke was directed (possibly by the Presbyterian minister of Millrow, Rev. John Ranken), to Thomas Thompson whom he promptly appointed to handle the Earl's affairs!

Antrim Episcopalians protested to the Dowager: 'Your own mind will at once feel the pernicious consequences of any power given to the people of Greenmount over your Ladyship's friends and affairs'. If Thompson wasn't stopped, they insisted (as if she didn't know it more than anybody), 'then all interest in this borough to any branch of your family is gone, and perhaps a residence here, if at any time in the future any of them should choose it'. The head and bearer of the family title had shown himself to be indifferent to the fortunes of his family. Antrim Castle itself was threatened. Where Cromwell and James 2 had failed, the 2nd Earl was succeeding.

The Dowager examined the power of attorney granted to Cpt. Clarke and discovered a technical error. This enabled her to delay forwarding the family deeds to Greenmount. She utilised this time to write to her son detailing the threat to his estates.

Hoping that his mother would now help settle his French debts, the Earl revoked the power of attorney. But the Thompsons, who had so nearly tasted political success, resolved to oppose the Massereenes at the next election.

1776 was an historic year. The Massereene bid to continue their parliamentary representation of Antrim borough was contested by Skeffington Thompson and fellow Independent, Alexander Stewart. William and Chichester Skeffington (brothers of the absentee Earl of Massereene) resisted the challenge. The result gave 164 votes each to the Massereenes and 134 each to the Independents. However, as the Massereenes were declared elected, the Thompsons lodged a protest. They complained that the aristocrats had exerted unfair influence and bribery during the election campaign. The special select committee which considered the petition censured the returning officer (Robert Clark) for ignoring minor irregularities, but vindicated the Massereenes and confirmed their election. Undaunted, having run the Massereenes close in the vote, the Thompsons redoubled their efforts for the next election.

Chichester Skeffington prepared for the 1783 election by raising a corps of Antrim Volunteers. The Volunteers call for a reform of the new and independent Irish Parliament appealed to the popular movement which supported the Thompsons. Skeffington's tactic was to win away that support.

Despite their industrial interests, the Thompsons found themselves poorly financed for the 1783 contest. Skeffington Thompson, hoping to achieve a compromise, wrote to William Skeffington suggesting that only one candidate from each side might stand for the two seats. The Dowager Countess exploited Thompson's blunder to the full. When she proposed publishing the letter so that the electorate should know that their popular spokesman, opposed to aristocratic influence, had tried to do a deal with the Massereenes, Thompson took the point and withdrew from the contest. The Massereene candidates again romped home at the polls with a decisive victory. (John O'Neill – created Baron in 1793 and Viscount in 1795 – was returned to represent Randalstown.) Upon taking their seats, the Massereenes supported the Commons' vote to reject the Volunteer Movement's plan for parliamentary reform!

By the 1790 election, it was the Massereenes who were facing financial difficulty. The Dowager Countess had always hoped that her £50,000 Row Tor Derbyshire estate would amply provide for her children. By 1785 she had been forced to sell most of it and was now considering selling off the remainder. Her security of tenure at Antrim Castle – and that of her sons (Henry, William and Chichester) – was threatened both by the estrangement between them and the eccentric earl, and his lordship's declared intention of returning to claim possession of the family seat.

If the Massereenes were to find financial security for the future they had to win parliamentary seats so that, in turn, they might acquire profitable government appointments. Were the Thompsons to accept such appointments, if elected, their popular support in the borough would desert them. Though an election which the Thompsons could well afford to contest would automatically cost the Massereenes what they could ill afford, the latter had no choice but to enter the fray. The stage was set for the final attempt to unseat the Massereenes, in the most remarkable elections of all.

Skeffington Thompson and Christopher Armytage Nicholson fought the 1790 election on the basis that the Irish Parliament in Dublin was unrepresentative. However, when William and Chichester Skeffington were declared elected, Thompson questioned the result. A select committee ratified William's election but did find Chichester guilty of pre-election bribery. Nonetheless, neither Thompson nor Nicholson were permitted to claim the seat now declared vacant.

A by-election was called. In the straight fight between Chichester and Skeffington, the Massereene defeated the Thompson by just 70 votes to 69! Thompson's inevitable objection was ruled out-of-order and dismissed.

That the Massereenes faced no opposition in the 1797 election was probably due to the unprecedented imposition, two years previous, of a £5-householding property qualification for voters. This effectively reduced Antrim's electoral roll from some 300 people to a mere 30 stalwart Massereene supporters.

Peaceful persuasion and the democratic process had been tried and found wanting, many contended. Ireland needed 'liberating' and the radical Protestants were no longer willing to be patient. There was a mood abroad for ending the country's troubles by resorting to arms. And the town of Antrim was on the eve of playing a prominent role in the formation of the United Kingdom.

'REMEMBER ORR'

William Orr was born in Milltown (while his father was purveyor of the troops at Shane's Castle), in 1766. In Duneane Parish Church, the youthful William married Isabella Greer. They raised their own family at Farranshane, Antrim.

Like the Thompsons of Greenmount, the Farranshane Orrs were Presbyterian Scots farmers and bleachers. The Thompsons' failures to politically defeat the Massereenes spurred on the creation of local branches of the countrywide Society of United Irishmen; 110,000 members in Ulster alone.

Inspired by the rebel Americans' Declaration of Independence (1776), and the Liberty which the revolutionary French citizens army had written (1789) with huge red flourishes, the United Irishmen sought the 'Liberty' of an Irish parliament not controlled by England, the 'Equality' that would arise in a social and political environment not dominated by the Established Church, and the 'Fraternity' which could be realised between Protestant and emancipated Catholic.

The secret Society of United Irishmen was presbyterian only in its politics, however. William Orr's Millrow minister – Rev. Alexander Montgomery (1791–1802) – protested at the secular spirit of the age: 'comparatively few attended public worship; the Sabbath was desecrated by political meetings'.[79]

The Episcopalian vicar of Antrim and Templepatrick – Rev. George Macartney (1773–1824) – was anxious to maintain the Ascendancy of his Established Church, (over Roman Catholic and Presbyterian alike). Son of a Scot who was five times Sovereign of Belfast (1759–1767), he had little love for the respectable, land-owning Presbyterian stalwart of Antrim's Masonic Lodge, William Orr. Macartney may have foreseen the argument, later propounded by Francis Joseph Bigger, that 'such would be the indignation of the people at the execution of a man like Orr that the foreseen insurrection of United Irishmen would be forced, the people taken at a disadvantage, and the country deluged in blood, so that in the anarchy of things, Castlereagh might evolve Pitt's favourite scheme of a union "when Ireland lay broken and bleeding".'[59]

Orr was a marked man from the moment Macartney read his article (in the United Irishmen's *Northern Star* journal) which demanded absolute political and religious equality and freedom for citizens of every creed and class; liberty rather than liberties, equality rather than privilege, fraternity rather than co-existence. As the local yeomanry captain, Macartney learned from two of his men that they had heard Orr administer the illegal secret oath of the rebels. On advising Dublin Castle about Orr, Macartney was empowered to issue an arrest warrant. Macartney's son – who had been hounded from Trinity College when fellow students discovered that he was informing against them – led a party of light horsemen (all of whom, it is said, subsequently died at the Battle of Antrim), to Milltown, where they apprehended Orr at his father's deathbed.

William Orr awaited trial in Carrickfergus Castle. Chichester Skeffington, as County Sheriff, was quickly accused of 'selecting' those whom he wished to sit as jury. The trial appears to have mocked justice. When the Viceroy offered: 'Mr Macartney, if you can lay your hand on your heart and say that you don't think the evidence is sufficient to convict the man, I will recommend his excellency to respite him,' Macartney refused (though he repented of this after Orr's execution). Lord Massereene – admittedly a man with an eccentric's reputation – once wrote of Macartney in a letter to the Viceroy: 'Oh, my lord, is it possible that government would ever confide a military department to this atrocious villain, a man than whom a more mad exists not out of Bedlam . . . For God's sake, my lord, above all things (let us not trust) an infernal monster like Macartney the vicar not of Jesus Christ, but of Satan'.

When the jury retired to consider the perjuries given as evidence against Orr, two (later reported that they) were threatened that if they did not agree the verdict must be 'guilty', they would face prosecution as United Irishmen. Another, who voiced concern about the proceedings, according to a contemporary report, 'was beaten and threatened with being wrecked and left not a sixpence in the world on his refusing to bring in a verdict of "guilty"'.[59]

The DYING DECLARATION

OF

WILLIAM ORR, of Ferranſhane, in the County of Antrim, Farmer.

TO THE PUBLICK.

MY FRIENDS AND COUNTRYMEN,

IN the Thirty-first Year of my Life, I have been sentenced to die upon the Gallows, and this Sentence has been in Pursuance of a Verdict of Twelve Men, who should have been indifferently and impartially chosen; how far they have been so, I leave to that County from which they have been chosen, to determine; and how far they have discharged their Duty, I leave to their God and to themselves.——They have in pronouncing their Verdict, thought proper to recommend me as an Object of humane Mercy; in Return, I pray to God, if they have erred, to have Mercy upon them. The Judge, who condemned me, humanely shed Tears in uttering my Sentence, but whether he did wisely in so highly commending the wretched Informer, who swore away my Life, I leave to his own cool reflection, solemnly assuring him and all the World, with my dying Breath, That that Informer was foresworn. The Law under which I suffer, is surely a severe one; may the Makers and Promoters of it be justified in the Integrity of their Motives and the Purity of their own Lives—by that Law, I am stamped a Felon, but my heart disdains the Imputation. My comfortable Lot and industrious Course of Life, best refute the Charge of being an Adventurer for Plunder: but if to have loved my Country, to have known its Wrongs, to have felt the Injuries of the persecuted Catholic, and to have united with them and all other Religious Persuasions in the most orderly and least sanguinary Means of procuring Redress:—If those be Felonies, I am a Felon, but not otherwise. Had my Councils, (for whose honorable Exertions I am indebted) prevailed in their Motion to have me tried for High Treason, rather than under the *Insurrection Law*, I should have been intitled then to a full Defence and my Actions and Intentions have been better vindicated, but that was refused, and I must now submit to what has passed.

TO the generous Protection of my Country, I leave a beloved Wife, who has been constant and true to me, and whose Grief for my Fate has already nearly occasioned her Death. I leave five living Children, who have been my Delight—may they love their Country as I have done, and die for it, if needful.

LASTLY, a false and ungenerous Publication having appeared in a Newspaper, stating, certain alledged Confessions of Guilt on my Part, and thus striking at my Reputation, which is dearer to me than Life, I take this solemn Method of contradicting that Calumny.——I was applied to by the High Sheriff and the Rev. William Bristow, Sovereign of Belfast, to make a Confession of Guilt, who used entreaties to that Effect; this I peremptorily refused; did I think myself guilty, I should be free to confess it, but on the contrary, I glory in my Innocence.

I trust that all my virtuous countrymen will bear me in their kind Remembrance, and continue true and faithful to each other, as I have been to all of them, with this last Wish of my Heart, nothing doubting of the Success of that Cause for which I suffer, and hoping for God's merciful Forgiveness of such Offences as my frail Nature may have at any Time betrayed me into. I die in Peace and Charity with all Mankind.

WILLIAM ORR.

CARRICKFERGUS GAOL,
OCTOBER 5, 1797.

N. B. *The above Declaration was made and read by WILLIAM ORR, in the Presence of the Rev. Mr. Savage.*

'Dying Declaration of William Orr' – Courtesy of H.M.S.O.

Twice the jury offered the verdict 'We leave him to your Lordship's mercy' before the hesitant 'guilty' was given. The judge is reported as weeping while he passed the automatic death sentence. When Orr was told that his life could be spared if he would admit his guilt, he refused:

> "I glory in my innocence. I am no traitor; I die a persecuted man. I die in peace and charity with all mankind."

William Orr walked to Carrickfergus Gallows Green on 14th October, 1797, having refused to travel in a coach accompanied by 'rude soldiers'. By all accounts, the affair has all the hallmarks of a judicial murder for a political end; the *London Courier* reported the execution: 'Murder Most Foul'.

Mourners lined the route of Orr's funeral procession through Ballynure and Ballyclare to the place of interment – his favourite sister's grave in the old

Templepatrick churchyard beside Castle Upton. The headstone beneath the old yew tree has never borne his name, through Orr's American descendants intimated recently, as we stood by the grave, their interest in having William's name engraved there.

A daughter (Willhelmena) was born to William Orr during the spring following his execution. Within seven weeks of her birth, thousands of United Irishmen, their ploughshares exchanged for pikes, bayonets and muskets, descended on Antrim town and castle, with the cry 'Remember Orr'!

THE BATTLE OF ANTRIM, 1798

> While close leagu'd crappies rais'd the hoards
> O' pikes, pike-shafts, forks, firelocks,
> Some melted lead- some saw'd deal-boards –
> Some hade, like hens in byre-neuks:
> Wives baket bonnocks for their men,
> Wi' tears instead o' water;
> An' lasses made cockades o' green
> For chaps who us'd to flatter
> Their pride ilk day.
>
> *'Donegore Hill,' J. Orr (1778–1816)*

In 'Donegore Hill', Ballycarry poet James Orr (William Orr's cousin), immortalised in Scots-Antrim dialect the United Irishmen who decided, in 1798, to take control of the most important military base on the road between Belfast and Derry – the town of Antrim.

It was the 31 years old Belfast textile manufacturer, founder of that city's first Presbyterian Sunday School and grandson of the founder of the *Belfast News Letter*, Henry Joy McCracken, who laid the contingency plans for the attack on Antrim.

Informers warned the Dublin government that trouble was brewing. Co. Antrim Governor, Viscount Lord O'Neill of Shane's Castle, immediately summoned his county's magistrates to meet in Antrim Market House on June 7 to arrange the introduction of martial law.

McCracken learned of the June 7 meeting and foresaw that if he attacked Antrim on that date he could clap O'Neill in irons, and all his magistrates.

On the evening of June 6, 1798, McCracken unfurled his flag (an inverted crown suspended from a gallows), at the old Roughfort, Craigarogan, a couple of miles from Templepatrick. According to one present: 'his eye beamed with the fire that animated his soul; a heart that was strong and knew no fear'. To his confederates in Derry and Donegal, McCracken issued his fiat:

> "Army of Ulster. Tomorow we march for Antrim. Drive the garrison of Randalstown before you and hasten to form a junction with the commander-in-chief.
>
> First year of liberty, 6th day of June 1798.
> Henry Joy McCracken, Commander-in-chief."

A copy of McCracken's dispatch found its way into the hands of Major Seddon, Commandant at Antrim Castle. He had only eighty weapons among a troop of dragoons and a dozen rounds of ammunition per man. Reinforcements from Military HQ at Blaris, Lisburn, were urgently requested.

A forced march from Blaris, commanded by Col. Clavering, was begun by the 2nd Light Brigade (composed of the 64th and a light batallion made up of the light companies of the [Armagh?], [Monaghan?], Dublin, Kerry, and Tipperary Militia) along with 150 of the 22nd Light Dragoons. With them they took two light six-pounder cannons and two howitzers. Col. Lumley led the advance guard of Clavering's force.

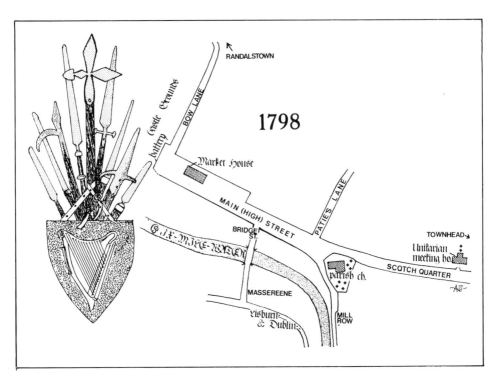

Antrim, 1798.

From Belfast, Col. Durham set out towards Templepatrick with 250 of the Monaghan Militia, a troop of the 22nd Light Dragoons and the Belfast Yeomanry Cavalry.

At 9 a.m. on June 7 the drums at Antrim Castle were beating the call to arms. When only forty of the town's civilian defence force (the yeomanry) reported for assembly at the castle, Seddon's dragoons searched the notoriously republican Scotch Quarter, and finding some two hundred of its Scots weavers missing from their homes set fire to seven of their cottages.

A small party of troops, having fought their way through a couple of hundred rebels near Kells, arrived in Antrim at noon with the news that the entire countryside around Antrim was moving with men bearing arms. The soldiers had escorted two magistrates from Ballymena who did not know that General Nugent had cancelled the magistrates' meeting at Antrim; nor did the United Irishmen know of the cancellation.

McCracken had marched about 500 men out of Roughfort and past the Four Towns Book Club at Roughfort Cross-roads to Templepatrick where they procured two old brass six-pounder cannons (though one proved unserviceable) which had been kept hidden beneath the pews of the meeting-house in the village. Musketeers formed the vanguard and behind the cannon (fixed to the wheels of an old chaise), trooped weavers, farmers and farmhands bearing old Volunteer flags, pikes, scythes and sticks. Fifers led them with tunes which roused the ranks. Mothers snatched away the little children who 'fell in' at the back of the grand 'parade'.

A handful of the rebels' leaders were dressed in suits modelled on the uniforms of the French National Guards: green jackets with gilt buttons (sporting the Irish harp minus any crown and a 'liberty cap' held aloof on a pike); some 'privates' wore a green sash or green ribbons pinned to shirts or green cockades.

With reinforcements from Carnmoney, Templepatrick and Killead, the insurgent army proceeded to the Antrim junction of the old Belfast Road and the road from Ballynure. Here they joined forces with their brothers from Larne, Ballyeaston and Ballyclare who had assembled during the night at Donegore Hill.

> An amusing illustration of their discordant union was exhibited when Larry Dempster, a Southern Roman Catholic and a deserter from the 24th Dragoons, was riding at the head of a rebel company from Ballynure on their way to the memorable conflict in the town of Antrim. Larry was flourishing a rusty sword in all the pride of his new office as an adjutant and surrounded by a number of his Protestant followers, when, forgetting the caution which had hitherto governed his utterances, he unguardedly exclaimed: 'By japers, boys, we'll pay the rascals this day for the Battle of the Boyne!' But Larry was quickly minded of his most untimely indiscretion. The blow of a pike, accompanied by a left-handed compliment to the Pope, laid him sprawling upon the road, where he made some rather unpleasant acquaintance with Presbyterian brogues.[71]

McCracken was disappointed that only about 3,500 men had 'turned out' – (many who had promised their support complained that morning of sudden attacks of gout!) – but he was thoroughly frustrated at the half hour delay caused by the mysterious pall of dense smoke seen rising from Antrim's Scotch Quarter that hot, sultry day. Henry Joy McCracken proudly pulled his helmet down over his loose, flowing locks, and addressed his followers:

> Men of Ulster! The hour has come for you to strike the first blow for Ireland and for liberty. Victory is certain! Musketeers, let every bullet find its mark! Pike-men, stand firm in the shock of battle, and let your trusty blades – forged for you by true and trusty men – be a wall of steel upon which, if our foemen rush, they rush to death. Follow me, my noble fellows, wherever I may lead you, and let our war-cry be, 'Remember Orr'!

McCracken proposed to lead the central division of his United Irishmen down Townhead Street (now Fountain Street) and through Scotch Quarter, there to rendezvous with a second column which John Storey of Islandbawn would move in by Patie's – (or Pedie's) – Lane (now Railway Street). When the castle militia engaged them in the town centre, a third column (of some 1,500 men expected from Randalstown) would move in along Bow Lane (Castle Street), and prevent any military retreat to the castle. But the half hour lost procrastinating about the Antrim fires had provided time for the advance guard of the Blaris troops to take up positions.

Without waiting for the arrival of Cols. Clavering or Durham, Col. Lumley had crossed over Massereene Bridge and, where Bridge Street issues out into Antrim's main street, his artillery men set up their two six-pounder cannons. They were flanked by the yeomen in an arrowhead formation. Other yeomen took up positions at the windows of High Street houses. They awaited the arrival (and confinement) of the rebels where the parish churchyard wall narrows the street.

Passing the Unitarian Meeting-House, Jemmy Hope's musketeers shattered the eerie silence with a volley of shots but to no effect except that Lumley's cannons bellowed replies and 'the artillery fired several rounds of grape shot with great rapidity, which, had their guns been judiciously laid, must have swept their opponents off the street; but so ill were they directed, that the only injury felt by the insurgents was their casting up some gravel in the street'.[76]

The clouds of smoke generated by the engagement, mingling with that from the cottages which still smouldered in Scotch Quarter, provided a dense cover which the rebels used to clamber behind the strategically-sited wall of All Saints' churchyard.

As the atmosphere cleared, Lumley led a furious cavalry charge towards the parish churchyard. It was then that Lumley discovered his enemy possessed a serviceable six-pounder brass cannon. Loaded with about 400 musket balls and a six-pound round shot, the cannon inflicted casualties among dragoons, artillery men and yeomen.

Cornet John Major was one of those who charged with Lumley (in Captain Sinclair's Troop of 22nd Light Dragoons) and later wrote of the incident:

> "The rebels met our charge with a rush of Pikemen and our Quartermaster – Charley Simpson – was piked and killed near me, poor fellow. It was a mortal engagement and lasted about twenty minutes. The whole engagement was a bloody one for they were Dissenters and fought with great stubbornness."

A government spokesman observed:

> "Having made the charge, near twenty of the dragoons were killed or wounded. However, they bravely cut their way through, returned and renewed the charge by the churchyard wall, after leaving seventeen men dead in the street, about thirty wounded, and forty horses killed, all in the space of about two minutes."[69]

A wounded horse had fallen on the rebels' cannon and knocked it from its chaise-mount. Finding that they could not get it remounted, Hope's musketeers opened fire on Lumley's renewed charge.

> The streets were filled with smoke; bullets were flying in all directions; while men, whose faces were perfectly black through having to bite off the ends of their cartridges, rushed wildly hither and thither.

Though hopelessly outnumbered, the cavalry attempted to fight off the pike-men with military swords and bayonets. But some pikes had three dagger-like prongs, placed at right angles to each other: one for striking as with an axe, another for stabbing, and the third – hook-shaped – for pulling men off horses and cutting bridles.

Lumley sounded retreat. Many fled along Bridge Street to the lough shore. Those without mounts desperately leaped from Massereene Bridge into the river, though at least one unfortunate was 'pierced through and through with pikes, and fell dead into the water, awfully mangled'. Some cavalry retreated to new positions in Bow Lane, safe behind the Market House. The yeomen sought the safety of the castle garden, behind its perimeter (Battery) wall.

'Peg Gordon, a huge masculine beggar-woman and a strong loyalist, on the offer of a large reward, rushed to the two abandoned military cannons, and, catching a fast grip of the muzzles, actually drew them from the churchyard to the castle garden gate, escaping unhurt.'[75]

John Storey's column, who had been too frightened to go as far along Patie's Lane as the main street, now advanced towards the castle's garden wall from Bow Lane. Volleys from the yeomen above drove them back. In the midst of this commotion, 1st Viscount (John) O'Neill of Shane's Castle was assassinated at the junction of Bow Lane and Market Square. Dr Morton (of 37 High Street; second house to the right of [old] High St. Presby. Ch.), hurried to the library at Antrim Castle where he prepared Lord O'Neill for the journey down river and across the lough to Shane's Castle, where the Viscount died ten days later.

While Vicar Macartney was frantically rowing across the lough to acquaint General Knox with the course of events at Antrim, his teenage sons, William and Arthur Chichester, were commanding a party of twenty yeomen who ventured into the main street and retrieved the military cannons. When these guns again roared into action, and (from The Battery, overlooking Market Square) 'Roarin' Tatty' fired her last historic shot which sailed over the town to crash down through the roof of the parish church, the United Irishmen retreated out of range.

Leaving Jemmy Hope in charge at the churchyard, McCracken led a special task force along the backs of the main street's houses towards the castle garden wall. Their sudden appearance so surprised the cavalry sheltering in Bow Lane that the latter fled towards the Randalstown Road. The Randalstown rebels, delayed by their struggle to take that town, were not to know that the cavalry who came charging towards them from Bow Lane were, in reality, beating a hasty retreat. The men from Randalstown (led by William Orr's brother, Samuel), broke ranks and nearly their necks too in taking to their heels across the fields.

The Battle of Antrim, 1798.

Antrim Castle lacked the men, weaponry and leadership to hold out for much longer. Though Col. Durham's force had now arrived at the Townhead, and could survey the town from its hill there, Durham concluded that Antrim had fallen to the rebels. Refusing to enter the town, Durham began shelling. Col. Clavering too had arrived but checked his troops on the Dublin Road about a mile from Massereene Bridge, unsure as to what has happening in the town.

When the loyalists, crouched behind the garden wall of Antrim Castle, began to talk of surrender, one of their number, Ezekiel Vance, a Quaker yeoman:

> "left the wall and hurried in the direction of the castle, seizing as he went the cloak of a young woman named Abagail O'Neill with the intention of carrying it on to the roof and waving it to and fro there that it might be taken as a sign that an energetic movement on the part of the Military might yet succeed. But Abagail did not relish the unceremonious interference with her garment, and so warmly remonstrated; when Ezekiel Vance bade her hold her tongue, for she would be in eternity in ten minutes – a remark that seemed probable of realisation when made, and which reconciled the young woman to her loss. On the roof, with the aid of a pike or pole, he waved the cloak. The incident appeared to be understood, and so he rushed from the castle roof . . . crossed the river, the water being low from drought, ran, still bearing aloft the cloak, met the Military, and conducted them into the town."[75]

As Durham's troops reached Scotch Quarter, some people fled from their homes. But the soldiers were at the backs as well as the fronts of their homes, and several men and women shared the fate of the weaver William Eckles, who 'rushed into the street, when he was struck by a bullet, threw up his arms, and fell dead'. 15 years old Jane Johnson was fatally shot in the arm when she ran to the aid of her dying brother, Arthur.

> In despair McCracken rushed forward himself as if he were going to charge the enemy alone; but two of his pikemen, crossing their weapons before him, tripped him in the dust . . . It was a trying moment for Henry Joy. Everything that talent and courage could suggest was attempted to restore order and revive the flagging courage of his men, but all in vain. They fled for their lives, actually bearing down in their wild flight the man who had proudly led them to victory.

45

Some two hundred rebels were cut down as they fled across the fields.

When Clavering and Lumley led the charge of the Light Brigade across Massereene Bridge, Jemmy Hope's 'Spartan Band' rushed from the parish churchyard to the town centre, feinted a counter-charge (which momentarily confused the military) and dashed off up Patie's Lane.

However, the sentries whom Durham had left at the head of the town barred the escape route to Donegore. With cannon to the front of them and cannon to the rear of them, the United Irishmen making for Donegore found themselves trapped in the open field of the hill overlooking Antrim. Wildly they fought – fatally wounding Col. Lumley – but only two hundred escaped (with magistrate Adair their prisoner) to rendezvous with Jemmy Hope and Henry Joy at Donegore Hill. The Redcoats pursued them, razing to the ground in the process the old home of William Orr at Farranshane and that of his cousin, James, at The Folly, Greystone.

The military commanders, who retired to the Massereene Arms Hotel, were dissuaded from their intention of setting fire to Scotch Quarter, though its homes and shops were ransacked and looted. Much of Templepatrick, however, was razed to the ground by the Monaghan Militia on June 8.

Three days after the conflict, when block-wheel carts began collecting about 300 rebel corpses (piled under the Market House) for burying in large holes on the Sixmilewater's south bank about a third of a mile from the lough, Ezekiel Vance believed he was watching cartloads of dead pigs passing on their way to Belfast. 'As one approached with its ghastly load, the driver seated on the top was asked by the yeomanry officer commanding the burying party, "Where the devil did these rascals come from?" A poor wretch raised his gory head from the cart and feebly answered, "I come frae Ballyboley." He was buried with the others.' Old Peg Gordon wasn't the only bargain-hunter to undress corpses. Military dead were interred in the sands at Shane's Castle.

By June 13, just a week later, with the United Irishmen having lost three major pitched battles – Antrim, Saintfield and Ballynahinch – the back of the uprising in Ulster had been broken. Rural bard of Ballynure, James Campbell (1758–1818), reflected:

> In '98 we armed again
> To right some things that we thought wrang;
> We got so little for our pains
> It's no worth mindin' in a song.

On July 17, 1798, the day the Irish Parliament passed its Act of Amnesty, Henry Joy McCracken was publicly executed at Belfast's Old Market House where, on 1st January, 1801, the legislative union of Ireland and Great Britain would be proclaimed.

McCracken was buried in St George's graveyard, Belfast. John Storey, too, was executed and decapitated at Belfast Market House and is remembered on the family headstone in Muckamore old burying-ground as 'John, who died for his country, 1798'. In the old Unitarian burying-ground in the middle of Antrim, one headstone reads simply: 'Here Lieth the Body of Wm. Eckles, who departed this life the 7 June, 1798, aged 46 years'. And Jemmy Hope eventually found his final repose in Mallusk old cemetery. (Ezekiel Vance lived happily to the end of his days and lies in the old Quaker graveyard at Moylena).

Ironically, the United Irishmen succeeded in bringing about the United Kingdom. With the 1800 direct-rule Act of Union, however, Britain effectively appointed herself the target for all future grievances in Ireland. 1798, with its militant, secret societies, had set a pattern!

MASSEREENE LEGACIES

When the Act of Union disfranchised the Borough of Antrim (a place of 382 houses with a population of 2,183), Henry, William John and Chichester Skeffington, brothers of the 2nd Earl, claimed equal shares in the £15,000 compensation which the Earl received under the Act. Commissioners agreed that the brothers had preserved the Massereenes' interests throughout the Earl's years of irresponsible, riotous living and awarded each brother £3,750.

All Saints' Parish Church and Mill Row.

Incensed at his brothers' action (and convincing himself that brother William was a United Irishman) the 2nd Earl made a will in which each brother got just one guinea and everything else went to Lady Massereene and her heirs. Having shamefully abused his first wife (a jailer's daughter), the 2nd Earl had returned to Antrim in 1797 with a mistress, Mrs Elizabeth Blackburn. When they married in 1804, the new Lady Massereene had deviously secured complete control over the Earl, his will and the family estate. 'Mrs Blackburn' was probably also the mistress of a young man from Killead (called Doran) – whom she later married – who, together with his father – a one-time Roman Catholic priest by the name of O'Doran who secured from the Earl the £500 p.a. Church of Ireland living at Killead – aided and abetted in schemes to disinherit the Massereenes.

With the counsel of the Irish Solicitor-General, Henry Skeffington (3rd Earl of Massereene) successfully contested the will – published upon his brother's death in 1805 – on the grounds of Lady Massereene's 'undue influence' over the late Earl. To her was awarded £15,000 capital and an £800 life annuity; to the traditional Massereene family was granted recognition of their right to the family estates.

1811 claimed the lives of both the 3rd (bachelor) Earl and brother William, and so the title passed to the youngest brother, Chichester Skeffington, then Collector of Customs for Belfast.

Lord Henry Chichester Skeffington, 4th Earl and 8th Viscount Massereene, had married (1780) Lady Harriett Jocelyn, daughter of 1st Earl of Roden. (According to the historian, F. J. Bigger, Earl Roden 'ruthlessly slaughtered the hundreds of unarmed peasants who had surrendered on the curragh of Kildare, well earning for his fencibles the name of "Jocelyn's fox hunters"'. Lady Harriett's husband, charged Bigger, was 'a man willing to oblige the powers that be in view of past favours and of future expectancies. It was he who arranged the jury which tried William Orr and it was under his personal supervision the execution was carried out'. Bigger concluded: 'It was a well-matched alliance – Skeffington-cum-Jocelyn.'[59] Bigger, incidentally, was the 7th son of a 7th son.).

Unhappily for the 4th Earl, he held the Massereene title for only five years and, unhappily for the Massereenes, his death without male issue also meant the demise of the earldom.

In memory of Chichester Skeffington, Viscountess Harriett and her daughter recorded his death and burial at Antrim Parish Church by erecting within the church its first unusual Massereene monument: weeping figures in classical dress upon a Greek pediment flank Harriett's inscription of 'the firmness, integrity and benevolence with which through the influence of religious faith he fulfilled all the duties of his various stations, and the Christian patience and resignation with which he closed the period of a life devoted in study and in pleasure to serve God and to do good'.

The unusual patent which had created the viscountancy of Massereene permitted the title, upon the 4th Earl's death, to pass to his only daughter, Harriett.

Antrim Castle – Courtesy of Ulster Museum.

FERRARD'S PLEASURE GROUNDS

'Some of the highest names on the list of the peerage were proud to be enrolled as suitors' to Lady Harriett Jocelyn Skeffington, noted Charles Henry O'Neill of Shane's Castle; 'Coronets were glittering in her train, by the Six-Mile-Water, and at the courts of the Viceroy and Sovereign.'[52]

One of the 'highest names' who set out for Antrim to woo the fair Viscountess Harriett was the 2nd Viscount Ferrard of Dunleer, Co. Louth; the Rt Hon. Thomas Henry Foster, only son of John, Baron Oriel (last Speaker of the Irish House of Commons) and Margaretta Burgh, Viscountess Ferrard (originally from Cumberland).

When Foster's carriage broke down on the way to Antrim he interpreted the event as an ill omen and returned home. However, Harriett's curiosity about he whom she called 'this faint-hearted knight at love's tournament who won not the fair lady' resulted in their happy marriage in 1810. Assuming by royal licence her ladyship's surname Skeffington, Foster became the 9th Viscount Massereene and Ferrard, Baron of Lough Neagh.

As an inscription on the front of Antrim Castle recorded, Foster extensively altered this 'old frowning keep' in 1813. He removed the northern wing's six pointed gables (of old-French chateau style) and the seventh (plain-turreted) gable. These were replaced with a castellated parapet wall terminating with two castellated towers at each side of the three-storey, rectangular mansion.

Sometime about this period (and probably not later than 1818), the grand arched entrance gate of solid oak, complete with warder's turreted lodge above and machinery for operating the gates, was constructed at the southern end of the castellated park wall. It has always been and must remain an important and romantic feature of Antrim's historic Market Square.

Above the gate, Antrim Castle's coat of arms is proudly displayed. The chevron between three chaplets (in the second and third quadrants) is the Clotworthy Arms; the three bulls' heads (in the first and fourth quadrants) are the Skeffington Arms. The family motto – 'Per Angusta ad Augusta' – translates 'through hard times to prosperity'.

Their grooms and stable lads acquired elegant quarters with the provision of the Neo-Tudor coach house and stables known as Clotworthy House (*c.* 1840). The arched gateway in the castellated front of the building was surmounted by an impressive clock. On either side, the sculpted heads of a good, God-fearing blind tenant and his ugly wife record a sermon in stone from the master-mason: the

Antrim Castle Entrance – Courtesy of Ulster Museum.

Almighty rewarded the pious man's craving for the gift of sight to behold the stunning beauty of his wife which, hitherto, he could imagine only from her graphic descriptions of herself; however, one look at his shrewish wife and the good man promptly prayed for the restoration of his blindness!

Favourite dogs and horses lie buried near the west (Flemish) gable of this 'Castle Farm' which so romantically fronted the old ivy-clad bridge leading across the Fir Field to the deer park of a thousand acres bordering Lough Neagh for some four miles.

While the present Lord Massereene's Chilham Catle Gardens were being laid out by Capability Brown, Lady Massereene in Antrim and her Lord Ferrard were proposing to restore the French character of the Stuart gardens about Antrim Castle.

The Pleasure Grounds of Antrim Castle were originally designed in the 17th century to echo, at almost every turn, something of Louis 14's Versailles Palace Gardens. 'Few towns have so splendid a park,' concludes Ernest Sandford in his N.I.T.B. book *Discover Northern Ireland* and continues, 'nor one containing so many interesting features.'

The hedges bordering the long ornamental fish ponds are now unique in Ireland: towering elms – sheltering and screening the ponds – thickly planted in line, interwoven, cut and dressed into gigantic hedges, as at Versailles. 'When the cascades are in full play,' noted one 19th century visitor, 'and the cascades rushing and bounding over the ledges and sparkling in the sunshine, the effect is beautiful.' (Unfortunately, little remains of the original limestone feature between the upper and lower ponds.)

In contrast to this area of ordered, civilized nature – a classic example of the popular improvement of estates according to 'picturesque' principles – another aspect of that emerging sensibility which we loosely call the Romantic movement characterised the heavily wooded area between the ponds and the perimeter wall next Antrim: 'The Wilderness' (37 acres), was landscaped in a sort of contrived irregularity, obscurity, wildness; its most charming feature was the 'Lovers' Progress': a romantic trail which featured 'introduction wells', 'senitmental paths', 'pouting arbours', 'declaration groves', 'Hymen's bowers' and, beside the broad unsecluded avenue leading from the large circular fish pond to the 'Terrace Gardens' – a 'divorce pond'! – now covered!

The 'Terrace Gardens', elevated some twenty feet above the park and reached by the (still existing) flights of stone steps, were, originally, rose gardens interspersed

Clotworthy House – Courtesy of Pat McGuigan.

with ornate urns with lawns for croquet which was 'played here by the fair denizens of the castle with grace and vivacity', observed Earl O'Neill in 1860. Later, four kitchen gardens with well-stocked greenhouses were located here. From the 'Wishing Stone' – (perhaps the same semi-circular 'wishing stone' now lying in the small burial-ground beside the long ponds?) – could be seen the 'Crow's Foot Five Vistas': All Saints' Church, the Round Tower, the Sperrins, Shane's Castle and, of course, the Castle-of-Antrim (as it should properly be called).

A better view would have been afforded from the summit of the old Anglo-Norman motte – 'The Mount'. It was the first Lord M. & F. who added its gently spiraling path, bordered by a manicured yew hedge. From the summit one could easily identify which path led out of the intricate labyrinth below, or catch a glimpse of the 'Giant's Organ' – a substantial reproduction of the famous Giant's Causeway feature, constructed from the distinctive hexagonal columns brought by cart from the Causeway. (Since military interference with this conversation-piece, during the last war, little more than the foundations remain; next the Randalstown Road wall.)

Between the river and the remains of the (1887) six-sided tower and billiards-room wall, a wide flight of steps still leads from the castle site to the lower terrace where a delightful rockery reached to the old ivy-clad bridge. Here were created artificial mounds, improvised bridges, arbours, tunnels, 'secret' flowerbeds with fine shrubs and ferns in fleur-de-lis patterns, and borders of fine red gravel imported specially from Holland; the haunt of fauns and nymphs and, surely, of Pan himself.

Lord Massereene and Ferrard survived his wife by a dozen years. After her death in 1831 perhaps he pondered anew on the inscription on his mother's memorial urn (now in Antrim Castle Grounds), in his old childhood home of Oriel Temple at Collon, Co. Louth, which records the celebrated Baron Oriel's reflections on the Collon estate's loss upon the death (1820) of his beloved Margaretta, the Viscountess Ferrard: 'This blessed retreat: chosen, planned, formed and finished by the refined and incomparable taste of its dear departed mistress. Where now is its boast? Its bright inhabitant is gone'.

From Collon, Lord Massereene had inherited two priceless treasures. As the last

Speaker of the Irish House of Commons, Baron Oriel had been the one to declare the Act of Union passed. With the end of the parliament, he took possession of the Mace and Speaker's Chair, shrewdly declaring: 'When that body which owned the Chair and Mace, and entrusted them to me, claims them from me I will return them'. Lord Massereene placed the Mace in the custody of the Ulster Bank, Belfast, and the Speaker's Chair – similar to the one at Westminster – was installed in Antrim Castle's Oak Room.

'The Oak Room is a unique apartment of large dimensions. The walls from floor to ceiling are wainscotted with solid Irish oak, chiefly of a dark shade, relieved occasionally with lighter coloured oak, elaborately carved, and formed out of trees from the park. Three windows opening on the river terrace, and numerous mirrors in massive oak frames, light up and enliven the appearance of this room. Armorial bearings and alliances of the family are painted in exquisite style on the panels. The chimney-piece at the lower end is in itself a study. It is of solid carved oak, and set with the grate in one frame. On touching a secret spring the entire of the massive frame swings out, and discloses a curious recess at the back for personal concealment which reminds us of the tales of knight-errantry – of gallant knights and forlorn damsels – the tournament and battles and sieges of old, when vaulted chambers and subterranean passages, with secret modes of exit, were the usual appendages to baronial hall and lordly castle. The ceiling is painted characteristically in light oak. Suspended on the walls are numerous family portraits in oil. These canvas memorials form a mystic reunion of companionship between the generations of the present and the past . . .

The furniture in this truly magnificent apartment is all 'en suite' of Irish oak, the chairs high-backed in the old style, and elaborately carved. But the all-absorbing feature of the room is the arched recess. In it rests the 'Speaker's Chair' of the Irish House of Commons, recalling to memory many a thrilling episode of the historic past of Ireland – Speaker Foster, Grattan, Flood, Castlereagh, Hussey Burgh, Yelverton, Fitzgibbon, O'Neill, Connolly, Curran, 1782, and the Union. The chair is of solid oak. The arms on it are formed out of one entire piece. The top is rounded into a half circle, and is elevated considerably over the head of the person seated in it. Above the chair, ranging round the dark oak wainscotted wall of the arched recess, are fifteen shields suspended, the arms painted heraldically, and in chronological order, of the various Speakers of the Irish House of Commons, commencing with Sir John Davies, the first Speaker, in the Parliament of James 1, in 1613, and ending with the Right Hon. John Foster, the fifteenth and last Speaker, in the year 1801. In the centre of this recess and over the chair are the arms of Ireland – the harp and the crown, and above them the arms in full of "Speaker Foster".'[52]

The Oak Room (which also sported the parish church's original oak door, riddled with bullets from the 1798 Battle of Antrim), was only one of a suite – featuring a French drawing room, library, breakfast and dining parlours – (above the river terrace) which, with their doors all opening into each other, offered a 156 feet long display of elaborate grandeur. Among the thousands of books were Cranmer's (1539) New Testament (an 1851 gift from the Cranmer family) and Queen Mary's Bible; rare manuscripts related to the Ulster Plantation, Charles 1's troubles, the 1641 Rebellion, Cromwell and the 1688 Revolution.

In 1843, Baron Oriel's grandson, John, inherited the castle and estates as the 10th Viscount Massereene and Ferrard; Baron of Lough Neagh; Viscount Ferrard and Baron Oriel of Collon, in the Irish peerage; and Baron Oriel of Ferrard in the U.K. peerage. His marriage to Olivia O'Grady of Limerick and Stillorgan Castle was celebrated as a union of the DeClotworthy and DeSkeffington Anglo-Norman barons with the Milesian O'Gradys of the Royal Irish House of Munster. His father had abandoned Antrim in 1834 to reside at Oriel Temple.

Lord John transformed Antrim Castle into a superlative mansion; graced by *objets*

The Oak Room, Antrim Castle – Courtesy of Ulster Museum.

d'art and elegant enough for a lavish reception to be held in 1856 to welcome His Excellency, the Earl of Carlisle. But Lord John would have preferred to be remembered as the composer of several poems on sacred subjects and an original metrical composition for the Psalms of David. As poet, he has left us:

> "Ireland! Yes, thou'rt a land of ire,
> of passion, and of endless strife;
> Of genius, which secretes its fire;
> of worth, scarce ushered into life;
> Of love, which breathes its soft desire
> in brawls; of scenes, with beauty rife;
> Of daughters, who must still appear
> too pure, too lovely for so wild a sphere."

Recumbent in the robes of a Knight of St Patrick, at prayer, under an elaborate high Victorian Gothic canopy, Lord John's effigy (commissioned by Lady Olivia, Viscountess Massereene and Ferrard), graces the parish church in Antrim.

Beside the spot in the Castle Grounds where Lord John stooped to pull up a young sapling, overbalanced and sustained a fatal injury, the Author fondly recalls 'discovering' a luminous white marble cross (in the dark passageway at the foot of the old steps leading from the lower terrace behind the castle site; 'The Sunken Garden'). Though the cross has been vandalised of late, the base still survives with the inscription: 'In Memoriam, John Viscount Massereene and Ferrard, April 18th, 1863'.

Viscountess Olivia, buried at Torquay in 1874, is remembered still in Antrim by her son's gift of a memorial window in stained glass and fitted (1890) to the north wall of All Saints' Church. That same son, the 11th Viscount, presented the adjacent window (1895) as a memorial to his three brothers.

* * * * *

High Street (east) – Courtesy of Ulster Museum.

On the eve of the 19th century, Antrim had 382 houses, Crumlin – 100, Doagh – 30, Randalstown – 51, Templepatrick – 30, and Toomebridge about 10. The numerous bogs in the barony of Massereene had been mostly cleared since 1772 and the district was generally distinguished for its rich harvests of oats, potatoes and flax.

The boom in agriculture enjoyed by local landowners during the long Napoleonic War ended suddenly with the peace of 1815; some lost their estates, like the Fergusons of Donegore, but others found new fortunes in industrialisation.

INDUSTRIAL REVOLUTION

A socio-economic revolution clattered and banged Antrim into the 19th century; its hub was centred on the Sixmilewater's plentiful (and approx. 100-horse-powerful) water supply which could be guaranteed at least nine months of the year.

The Massereenes had a large corn mill at Mill Row (Riverside Nos. 60-62) which received corn dried locally according to the following practice:

> "A fire was lighted against a wall or ditch; branches of trees were placed in a slanting position against the top of the wall or ditch; over these wheat straw was closely spread, and upon that a layer of grain was spread, which, when it was dried by the heat, was carefully brushed down the straw into a winnowing-sheet, and replaced by a fresh layer of grain."[80]

Next door, the Ferguson family had rebuilt the paper-manufacturing mill (estbd. 1776); the paper was principally used by the linen bleachers for packing, lapping and ornamenting their products:

> "The paper mill consists of two separate houses situated near the brewery. One of these contains a paper machine (one of the first introduced into this country) and three engines for masticating the rags. The house is 38 feet high. The dimensions of the wheel which propels the machinery is 10 feet in diameter, and 3 feet 6 inches broad. It is a breastwater wheel. The other houses contain machinery connected with the finishing of paper, which is propelled by two breastwater wheels one of which is 16 feet in diameter and 5 feet broad."[20]

Other paper mills had been established at Dunadry (Daniel Blow's), Randalstown (Francis Joy's), and at Bog Head but this last enterprise found that it could not compete with the Fergusons' successful concern.

The cotton spinning industry in Belfast encouraged domestic calico weaving about Antrim. When the industry was mechanized on a large scale in Lancashire, however, Antrim's weavers, by the 1830s, found the competition crippling and switched to the more demanding art of linen weaving. A few, like J. Ferguson who operated a mill at Crumlin, had begun spinning flax as early as 1812.

53

High Street (west) – Courtesy of Ulster Museum.

The texture of life for rhyming weavers spinning yarns in the chimney corners of their thatched, rough-cast cottages was often lined with webs of intrigue:

> "Diverse persons of the town of Antrim who rent loom seats and hire looms in their own houses to poor weavers who has them not of their own at a rate a week as agreed on between them and the weaver, and . . . by the negligence of the owners of such looms, they let the rent rise to a considerable amount to which the weaver perhaps is incapable of paying, they will then seize on, or detain the web, though not the weavers property."

Antrim and district was soon being hailed as Ireland's most extensive bleachgreen with 'nearly one half of the adult male rural population . . . engaged in the manufacture of the linen'.[20]

The Ordnance Survey of 1838 (which was suspected at the time as being a crafty government 'cover' for a search for valuable minerals!) made a detailed inventory of the great water-wheels which provided the locomotive power behind the Vale of Moylena's roaring landscape:

> "The beetling mills are in the townland of Moylinny and are the property of William Chaine esq . . . The machinery of one is contained in a house 50 × 33 feet and is propelled by a breast water wheel 22 feet in diameter and 6 feet broad. The machinery of the other is contained in a house 52 feet × 38 feet and is propelled by an undershot water wheel, 17 feet in diameter and 12 feet broad. Fifty-two acres of spreadfield attached to those mills are in this parish.
> Greenmount bleach mills are in the townland of Tirgracey on the property of William Chaine esq. The houses are two storey and three storey high, slated and in excellent repair. The water wheel of the mill is 16 ft in diameter × 4½ ft broad. It is a breast wheel. The water wheel of the second mill is 12 ft in diameter × 3 ft 9 ins. broad. The water wheel at the Boghead mill is 15 ft in diameter × 6 ft 4 ins broad . . . the fall of water to all these mills is 19 ft.
> The beetling engine and wash mills in the townland of Shanoguestown are propelled by two breast wheels, one of which measures 22 ft in diameter by 6 ft broad. The other measures 20 ft in diameter by 5 ft 6 ins broad and the fall of water is 19 ft.
> The washing and beetling engines in the townland of Muckamore are propelled by three breast water wheels. One of these is 15 ft in diameter by 16 ft broad, the second is 15 ft in diameter by 4 ft broad and the third is 14 ft in diameter by 3 ft broad.
> The beetling engine of Mr William Beck is in the townland of Islandbawn. There is a breast wheel here measuring 15 ft in diameter × 3 ft broad. There is a second breast wheel measuring 16 ft in diameter by 3 ft broad and a third of the same dimensions. The fall of water for these wheels is 14 ft. There is a bleaching green attached to these mills."[20]

As well as bleaching greens, little villages sprang up around these mills: at Riverside, where Alexander Ledlie converted the corn and flour mills, and the Boals transformed (1888) the old paper mill (which had lately operated as The Celtic Paper Company) into a weaving factory; at Bog Head (where the workers' homes were razed in the early 1960s); at Muckamore, where a village community still survives in

Vale of Moylena.

the terraced mill houses; and at Dunadry, where something of Daniel Blow's old mill (which switched to linen manufacture) and the mill manager's house survives amid the modern hotel excellence of the Dunadry Inn (though a recent slum clearance scheme effectively erased the old village).

Two high-pressure engines (300 h.p.) and one (100 h.p.) turbine water-wheel produced heavy or 'medium' yarns at the Cogry Flax Spinning Company's thirty acre complex at Doagh. Victorian rural Ulster in general, and everyday life about Doagh, Cogry and Kilbride in particular, are vividly and superbly brought to life in Florence Mary McDowell's books, *Other Days Around Me* and *Roses and Rainbows*.

'Old Bleach Linens' brought international fame to Mssrs. C. J. & R. T. Webb's Old Bleach Linen Company at Randalstown. During structural alterations to these buildings and their mill-races it was discovered that this 15 acre site had once been quarried by primitive man as an iron works. 'Ironworks', or Randalstown as it was renamed, had a population of 868 in 1881.

Glenoak mills – the first flour mills in the north of Ireland – built at Crumlin in 1765 were destroyed by fire in 1884. The 40 acre site was rejuvenated two years later, however, when the Ulster Woollen Co. installed 25 looms worked by a Hercules turbine water-wheel and 100 h.p. steam engine. The Crumlin (or Camlin) river supplied ample water for the manufacture here of serges, flannels, worsted coatings, friezes, fingering and knitting yarns, and the famous 'Lough Neagh Tweeds'.

A golden era? One must murmur, sadly, that the days of the mills were also unnatural ones: little children slaved from six in the morning to six at night 'for buttons', beside pregnant mothers who stood at their looms until natural labour forced them home. Working in clouds of flying particles of tow, few mill workers were without a racking cough.

The mill-race which accompanies the Sixmilewater down through the romantically luxuriant Vale of Moylena has lost little of its power, though the machinery of the noisy beetling mills has long since fallen silent. Most of the neat little cottages scattered through this wild, winding valley have gone, though, here and there, a few nestle still among the beeches and sycamores to delight the eye of the rambler.

The delight of a visit to Moylena Valley as it was in the early 19th century is recorded in S. C. Hall's *Ireland*:

> We have never seen pastoral beauty so happily combined with the beauty of industry . . . The high-road traveller, much as he may admire the widespread bleach-greens, the taste and elegance of the various residences in their immediate neighbourhood – the clean, well-dressed, homely, and happy

appearance of the inhabitants – can form no idea whatever of the graceful recesses of this sylvan spot. It is unrivalled in its way – trees, rocks, banks, and paths screened from the sun, and terminating in vistas revealing the fine country beyond, while at your feet the waters rush to their trained courses. It would be impossible to describe the varied, yet continued beauty of this scene: the river twists in the most fantastic manner, and Mr William Chaine has availed himself not only of the vast water power, but has erected his bleaching machinery where it least disturbs the aspect of the whole.

Today's visitor – whether he be a naturalist, industrial archaeologist, rambler or simple romantic – when he follows the lane from the Belfast Road through Muckamore Forest Nursery to the river, or strolls by the old mill-race from Muckamore itself along Moylena Banks, will find himself in the midst of Moylena's enchantments. Beyond the waterfall, a old rustic bridge crosses the Sixmilewater, just below the weir; an idyllic pastoral environment graced with the impressive ruins of one of the old beetling mills, still with its majestic waterwheel; the air no longer saturated with ammonia and graphite. And everywhere as W. S. Smith observed:

Beeches, horse-chestnuts, Scotch firs, alders, sycamores, larches, ashes, wild cherries, hazel and hawthorn bushes intermingle, and constitute generally a soft, varied, luxuriant scene, truly delightful to look upon. When the hawthorn bushes are covered with their milk-white flowers, when the wild cherries are in bloom, and the horse-chestnuts have put out their spikes of cream-coloured, waxy, sweet-scented flowers; when among the underwood are hundreds of male-ferns throwing aloft their graceful, feather-like fronds, and the declivities are adorned with bright gems scattered by Flora's bountiful hands, this portion of Moylena Valley is truly picturesque, and very pleasing to behold.

Nor is it beautiful in spring-time only. It is beautiful when clad in the rich robes of summer, when their various shades of green dissolve one into another; it is beautiful in autumn, when nature's drapery has changed its hues, and the Great Artificer has painted it red here, russet there, and golden yonder, or when the leaves, fit emblems of man's mortality, are falling and mingling with the earth; and it is grand, if not beautiful, even in winter, when rude Boreas enters it and sways wildly to and fro the bare trunks of the tall trees, and fiercely lashes about their long, leafless arms. It is grand also on a quiet, frosty evening, when those same trunks stand motionless and solemn, almost spectral, and those limbs are still as death, and fringed with beautiful snow.[28]

The local linen and yarn markets are brought back to life for us in the rough couplets of mid-Antrim rural bard, Hugh McWilliams (1831):

Behold the yarn market! look what's there
Of amiable females fine and fair,
With bunches that their arms can scarcely span
And others with a few rough dozen run.
The cautious purchaser withholds a while –
Cheap! he exclaims – bad stuff, and gives a smile.
The seller now retaliates again,
No better stuff, or yarn was ever spun.
I've fifteen spangle. And I'll beat a crown
There's not a bunch superior in the town.
In six short weeks, the servant maid and I
Spun what you see, 'twould be a sin to lie.
The bargains closed, he pays without delay
She counts it, puts it past, and turns away.

We'll now proceed to where the cloth is sold –
Behold that throng of people young and old,
With webs in readiness – it strikes the hour,
See how they forward rush with all their power
Towards the merchant, whom they well can tell
The quality of what they have to sell;
He views and turns the piles so quick, and then
Bids them a price, and with his ready pen
Claps on a mark immediately, and
Another's waiting, reaching out his hand . . .

Textile manufacture around Antrim created an important middle class which promoted the development of the town throughout the 19th century.

Market Square, Antrim – Courtesy of Jackie Peacocke.

DOWNTOWN NINETEENTH CENTURY ANTRIM

It is a sobering thought that after two or three hundred years the spelling mistakes of a couple of Antrim stonemasons are as plain today as when they were made: the Massereene & Ferrard crest above the gate of Clotworthy House ought to read 'Per Angusta Ad Augusta', instead of the nonsensical 'Per Augusta Ad Augusta'; an afterthought about the spelling of 'built' is a prominent feature of one of our country's richest classical buildings – Antrim Court House (see Datestone).

Many's the midnight thief who ended up in the dock at Market Square a couple of hundred years ago; smugglers too, in the shape of mill-proprietors charged with breaches of the revenue laws; or a spirited back-room operator who had tenderly concocted a savage dram of peasant firewater.

Northern Ireland's oldest courthouse, still in use, was built in 1726 following an application to the County Grand Jury by the Hon. John Skeffington. Lord Ferrard, who had the building repaired in 1817, added the crowning touch with that distinctive, octagonal cupola on its roof. The original building's rough masonry can still be seen through one of the upper windows on its northern side.

It's a wonder anyone ever appeared at the petty- or quarter-sessions during the last century if the writer of the ordnance survey memoir of the day is to be believed:

> "The Chief Constable is rarely effective, being most of his time absent or unwell, and might as well be anywhere else as he has no duty to do, or rather does no duty farther than connected with the payment or management of the affairs of his men."[20]

A generation later, Alexander Irvine noted:

> "Towards the close of a fair-day, when tongues are loosened, and men hanker as only men of Antrim can hanker for something sensational with which to wind up a glorious day – what more natural than twenty-four fists flying in all directions. All at it all at the one time, all bent on making an impression. No men armed with false knuckles or shillalahs. Just the common horny hands of toilers doing with their might what their hands found to do!"[88]

From the courtroom, a spiral staircase led to old look-out positions in the attic. Beneath the courtroom was a market place, and outside was the market square for the great fairs which spilled over into the high street.

'The numbers who attend the fairs are very great,' noted the O.S. writer, and, he admitted, 'as they are chiefly for amusement, they present towards evening disgraceful scenes of drunkenness and brawling.'

As the cocks crowed-in each new year of the last century, the farming community about Antrim congregated around Market Square for the annual livestock fair. About 150 cows would be auctioned and there were upwards of 400 pigs to choose from. A horse 'of middling description' could fetch £10.

The great local horse fairs of the century, from 1812 onwards, were staged at Ballyclare and Holestone; dealers were attracted from as far away as Scotland, England and Dublin. Connemara gypsies with colourful caravans always came to trade their ponies and donkeys.

Around 1840, ninety-five local farmers established the Antrim Union Farming Society and instituted annual 'cattle shows' at the Castle Farm (behind Clotworthy House). Competition prizes were awarded for ploughing, digging, crop growing, and especially 'thorough draining'; three local farmers were regarded as pioneers of such draining – Ballyhenry's Joseph Gilmour, Samuel and Arthur Molyneaux. Their success attracted the benevolent interest of the Royal Agricultural Improvement Society of Ireland who offered medals and money prizes at the shows. Lords Massereene, O'Neill and Templetown took keen interest in the Society.

The 1845 Cattle Show Report by Rev. James Çarley, minister of Antrim Old Pres. Meeting-Ho. (who was himself an exhibitor and winner of several prizes) records an entry of '110 beasts; also sheep, pigs, horses, butter and cheese; grain, turnips, carrots, rape, mangel, cabbages'. One cabbage weighed 50 lbs! The report concluded with an exhortation to the members to use every endeavour to improve stock and crop of every description.

Southwards from Antrim along the lough shore stretched what was called the Great Wheat Belt of Ulster. The farmers there were noted innovators, being the country's first to use threshing machines. The 1793-1815 French and British wars had acted as a catalyst to boost local agricultural prices – particularly grain. The deliberate encouragement of tillage helped landowners to break down the Scots and Irish rundale farming practice. However, if all this was at the expense of pasture, competition from American grain in the 1870s boosted a general changeover to a livestock-based agricultural economy. Most smallholdings were amalgamated and turned over to grass.

As well as Antrim's three grand annual markets in the latter half of the 19th century, there were monthly fairs and, after 1860, general-produce markets every Thursday. Local farms supplied potatoes, oats, turnips and cabbages.

> "The main street was lined with stalls which were crowded with gingerbread and candy. Petty merchants came from far and near to display their wares. Farm hands – male and female – changed their masters or made new contracts on that day, and hiring was done in the open street. The whiskey places did a roaring business; so did the peelers.
> Farmers brought cattle, pigs, fowl, grain and hay. It was a great day for beggars, wanderers, thimbleriggers, acrobats, conjurers and queer people who lived by their wits. I remember a time when my greatest ambition was to be old enough for a farmer to lay his hand on my shoulder and ask me to serve him for the following year! It was exciting to see a farmer bid a bargain with a boy, by spitting in his hand and slapping a shilling into the palm of the new farm-hand for the following year."[88]

The 'petty merchants' sold old clothes, cakes, fruit, woollen stockings, footwear, crockery, tinware and ironmongery. Servants and 'hands' were obliged to be hired in May-sunshine or November-bleakness, all their world wrapped in brown paper parcels stuck in their oxters. Men lined the sides of High Street, carrying rods (the 'for hire' symbol). Spittle-cum-hand-slapping may conjure up romantic-rustic images but the 'hiring ground' was truly a slave market.

Perhaps the inevitable disputes and assaults of an Antrim Fair Day prompted the legal profession to choose Thursdays as the time to throw open the doors of the Court House for petty sessions. Few paused on the double flight of stone stairs to admire the Florentine style of the Court House; under a sketch of the building, drawn by C. R. Cockrell, this notable classicist recorded: 'The roof has a good pitch, but it must be confessed that the dripping of the eaves is excessively inconvenient – the flight of steps is rendered almost impassable by the wet!'

Beneath the courtroom, the 'weigh-house' market place – a corridor of sorts: seven feet wide and running the entire length of the building – shared the ground

'Frenchman's House' (left) next to old R.I.C. Barracks, Castle Street.

floor with 'a wretched little cluster of filthy barbarous cells fronting the Market-place'.[17] The arrangement can still be plainly seen in the design of the various legal offices occupying the ground floor today.

From c. 1836, the R.I.C., stationed at 'The Yews' (No. 5 Castle Street; still standing), used the Court House cells as a temporary bridewell (until new barracks were completed, in 1856, at No. 23, Market Square; connected to the Market [and Court] House by an underground tunnel).

Only an iron railing separated the prisoners of those 'filthy barbarous cells' from the public in Market Square; 'the narrow space between this and the cell-doors is an apology for an airing-yard, and serves for both males and females; the cell for male prisoners is both day-room and night-room, and has two deal bedsteads; a small cell for drunkards adjoins, and holds fast for 48 hours each convicted drunkard who cannot pay the adjudicated fine'.[17]

Vagrants also tended to spread infection and disease. Though a dispensary was established in 1817 (with others at Crumlin, Doagh and Randalstown), and greatly improved conditions in the area, there were situations it could do little to combat: 'It would appear,' notes the O.S. Memoir, 'that Antrim's inhabitants have been contaminated by their intercourse with strangers as there are at present twenty-eight illegitimate children of various ages residing in it'.[20] Such children were usually abandoned and, eventually, taken in to the care of the Antrim Poor Law Union Workhouse (which building would later serve as Massereene Hospital).

The Workhouse had been established in the wake of a fierce cholera epidemic in the town. Entire families perished and the victims were quickly buried, far from the town: in the 'Spittle Field' between the Greystone and Moylena roads. Mill Row minister, Rev. Robert Magill – who lost his first wife and son in the epidemic, along with forty members of his congregation – compiled the following obituary for his 1839 congregation: 'inflammation 10, consumption 9, frailty 7, pox 6, burned 2, chincough 2, a fall 1, killed in mill 1, cancer 1, misent fever 1, croup 1, sore throat 1'.

Though the Board of Governors first met in 1840, the opening of Antrim Poor Law Union Workhouse on 19 September, 1843, was timely for some: within a year or two the population of Ireland was to be decimated by the 'Great Famine' (1845–49). The remains of 'famine walls' are still to be found locally.

The Workhouse's Infirmary Building and office block were completed by 1843 but the (front) fever hospital, with accommodation for forty in the main building and a further forty-five in the 'fever sheds', was not ready until 1847.

7,274 paupers were admitted to the Workhouse during its first decade of operation. 1,051 inmates died there, and were interred in the Paupers' Graveyard at the rear.

In its initial days of operation, women were set to spinning flax though, subsequently, wool was spun; men were engaged in stonebreaking. Entries in the Board of Guardians' Minute Book reveal that the notorious 1845 began conventionally enough:

The medical officer having reported that John Dubois, an aged pauper, admitted on the 21.1.1845 had died on the morning of the 23rd inst. from the effects of long exposure in being conveyed to the workhouse, and it having been ascertained that such delay had arisen from the person in charge having become intoxicated on the road . . .[19]

The Workhouse, Antrim.

As potato crops fail, however, the Minute Book records dinners of oatmeal and 'stirabout'. The menu for October 1845:

> In consequence of the contractor being unable, from the prevailing disease in the potato crop, to procure the full supply of a sound description –
> On Sunday, adult paupers to be allowed 7 oz. of oatmeal and children 3½ oz. with the usual quantity of milk;
> On Monday, Wednesday and Friday, adults to be allowed 4 lb. of potatoes each and children under 9 years 2 lb. each with usual quantity of milk;
> On Tuesday, Thursday and Saturday, adults to be served with ½ lb. bread and children ¼ lb. with the usual allowance of soup.

The Society of Friends rallied to help and each church actively assisted the poor in its congregation. October 6, 1847, was designated by the Mill Row (First Antrim) Presbyterian congregation as 'a day of humiliation and prayer' on account of the failure of the potato crop. Church records for the year speak of fever at epidemic proportions and the Workhouse's fever hospital filled.

Anna and Jamie Irvine of Pogue's Entry – who lost their second child during the 1847 epidemic – told their son, Alexander: 'As the ravages of the famine spread, nearly every family in the town mourned the absence of some member. Men and women met on the street one day and were gone the next'. Certainly, this may have been true of the very poor folk – particularly those crowded in the mud huts of Massereene – who constituted about a fifth of the population.

Generally, however, like the rest of Ulster, the linen industry saved Antrim during the Great Famine. By weaving linen the rent could be paid, the family income not being wholly dependant on agricultural labour; (see also 'O.S. Table of Trades and Occupations, 1835–38'[20]).

By 1853, Antrim Workhouse, which had been built to accommodate 965, had only 180 inmates remaining. In the quarter-century following the 1841 census (which recorded a local population of 5,182), the parish population figures fell to 2,138, and continued to fall (1,647 in 1881) – many emigrating to the United States of America – until the end of the century; 1891 census: 1,965.

The Towns Improvement Act of 1854–55 allowed for nine of the town's most respected gentlemen to act as Town Commissioners. In 1888, William Vance was elected chairman for commissioners J. Kirk, W. Williamson, W. D. M'Manus, Thos. Bigger, Rt. Johnston, D. Weir, W. Armstrong and J. Storey.

For the churches, however, the 19th century was one of unparalleled freedom and growth. The vicar of Antrim (and personality of 1798), Rev. George Macartney, borrowed £1,500 for the parish church in 1812 and architecturally dominated the town with the skyscraping square embattled tower to which, four years later, was added the elegant octagonal steeple (or spire) which remains to this day the most prominent feature of the Antrim skyline. The church was given a new roof in 1825.

Rev. Macartney was buried in the churchyard in 1824. His elder son, Rev. Arthur Chichester Macartney, served as a captain of artillery at the siege of Flushing and in the Peninsular War. From 1821 until his death in 1843 he was Vicar of Belfast. His younger brother, Joseph, was the Belfast attorney who acted in negotiating the leases with the tenants of the 2nd Marquis of Donegall.

During the persecution of the previous century's Penal Days, Roman Catholics celebrated mass at the open-air venues of Tornarush (Drumsough), Kilbegs (Milltown Cemetery) and at Magillstown racecourse on the Randalstown Road.

ST COMGALLS, ANTRIM

Ross 82

St Comgall's R.C. Chapel, Antrim.

£1,400 subscribed in 1818 enabled Father Bernard McAuley to erect the first chapel in Antrim. Half a century after its consecration it was succeeded by the new St Comgall's Church (1870), which added another distinctive tower to the town, at the Castle Street-Oriel Road junction. (After another half century, the early 19th c. Wilderness Lodge, at the opposite corner of this crossroads, became the Sisters of St Vincent Convent).

For the middle of the century, church attendance figures in Antrim reveal: Parish Church – 300; 1st Antrim Presbyterian – 800; High Street Presbyterian – 225; Roman Catholic – 700; Wesleyan – 75; Primitive Wesleyan – 75; and Quakers – 18.

Sundays, then, began on Saturdays. Blue coats with brass buttons, fustian trousers and black hats for the menfolk, meticulously prepared. 'Sunday best' was pressed and boots buffed, and the rice pudding baked or boiled. Cleanliness and Godliness. Of course, strict observance of the Sabbath did not preclude attendance at the alehouse (often erected beside the church building); to accommodate rejoicers, services would be arranged with 'intermissions'. The Moat Inn (beside St John's, Donegore), for example, was popular both during and after church meetings.

The Millrow Presbyterians were now so numerous that despite the gallery and extension added to their meeting-house a new building had to be erected (1834–37). The latter – about 100 yards east of the old and with access to Church Street – was accidentally burned to the ground early in 1860; during its rebuilding, services were

First Antrim Presbyterian Church.

conducted in the Courthouse. Though the interior was much altered in 1903, the exterior of the rebuilt church – with its huge doric columns, copied from sketches of a Greek portico at Thoricus – has changed little in the past century.

Church Street, in 1838, acquired the gate of the former meeting-house at Mill Row, where the legendary William Orr of Farranshane had worshipped; as had David Kinlay 'who showed King William the pass on the Boyne on the day of the battle', according to the register of the (1820–39) minister, Rev. Robert Magill. Magill's Diary contains his delightful artistic impressions of many in his congregation. When Magill's remains were exhumed from Templepatrick and reinterred at Donegore, that (Unitarian) 'rival' contemporary, W. S. Smith, quipped: 'He was married twice and buried twice!'

Former Methodist Church, Antrim.

Magill's successor, Rev. Chas. Morrison (d. 1890; buried at Edinburgh), who built Ashville, offended sufficient of his congregation in 1850 for enough families to withdraw and establish the High Street Congregation, attached to Ballymena Presbytery. Its minister was Rev. J. H. Orr. In our time, this congregation has moved to a beautiful, though isolated, modern church building at The Steeple.

Gladstone's disestablishment of the Church of Ireland, 1869, at first did little to heal the old and turbulent Anglican-Presbyterian dissensions. For Muckamore's Church of Ireland congregation, St Jude's Parish Church was built in 1842, for £2,000; the Rectory was a gift from Greenmount's Thompsons.

The Methodist Chapel (now a branch library), was erected opposite Pogue's Entry in 1805. The Primitive Wesleyan Methodist Chapel – the 'Antrim Discount Stores' of 1980s – was built in 1823 at a cost of £200. In 1882, the renowned Sir Charles Lanyon laid the foundation stone, at 76 Church Street, of the Masonic Hall; the Antrim Lodge was formed in 1776.

Sunday-schools and charitable societies endowing day schools contributed to the moral and intellectual education of Antrim's children. In 1812, Viscount Massereene helped to erect the Episcopalian endowed schoolhouse of Erasmus Smith, (the 17th century English merchant-adventurer), in Bow Lane, (Castle Street).

One who enrolled in this parochial school during the latter half of the century was Alexander Irvine who reported that 'the pedagogue of that period delegated his pedagogy to a monitor, and the monitor to one of the biggest boys, and the school ran itself'. A very different picture is painted by F. M. McDowell ('Other Days Around Me') and by the 'teacher' (dressed in period costume!) in the restored National School at the Ulster-American Folk Park, Omagh.

Opposite The Well entry (at the side of Sean Byrne's shop), No. 2 Fountain Street still sports a plaque which boasts: 'Antrim National School, 1841'. One who experienced national schooling in Antrim writes:

"It was one apartment, like a large church hall, with high arched roof, and windows eight feet from the floor, so our only view was of grey cement walls. The only heating in winter came from an old-fashioned fireplace with thick iron bars, most of the heat going up the chimney. There were between one hundred and one hundred and twenty scholars, from infant class to second sixth, with sufficient desks to seat only half the number, while the other half stood in four classes round the sides of the room.

A semi-circle was drawn in white chalk on the floor with crosses where pupils were to stand to attention, with feet together and slates and books in straps at our feet. The lessons began with questions on our homework and the quality of that was rewarded by going up to the top of the class, or vice-versa for poor answering, so a continuous movement went on till that part was over. Then came writing on slates which were icy cold in winter so that sometimes we could hardly write. Every half hour there was a general post, with more writing, on paper, at the desks. Only the lucky few who were near the fire felt any heat. There was plenty of slapping with the cane, which kept the Master busy. Indeed it was quite the thing, and if one was too good to require an occasional slap – well, one heard about it. The head-master was partly paid by fees, five shillings each per term, for those who could afford that sum and less for others not so fortunate, plus one shilling for the use of ink, pens and slate, pencils, and one shilling for fuel during the winter term. We bought our own slates, copy, dictation and school books. The slates with a wooden frame were easier to hold in class, as the sharp edges were liable to poke into one's tummy. We had an hour for lunch, when the school door was locked. The lucky ones who lived nearby went home; the rest of us played about, just as children do now."

Grace C. Bonthrone,
'Childhood Memories of Co. Antrim.'

Grace (née Gaston) travelled by 'pony and croydon' to school each day from her father's Beech Cottage farm in Milltown village. Beech Cottage – now the home of Mr and Mrs Peter Cosgrove – remains largely as Grace described it, most of it being more than 300 years old.

A daughter of Rev. W. S. Smith together with solicitor William Williamson's son, though they both lived within a few yards of Master Savage's Fountain Street National School, attended Mrs Scott's National down at Mill Row. And in lower Church Street, the Wesleyan Mission operated a school. Among individuals offering tuition in their own homes were two advertising a 'Classical English and mercantile education'. Nathaniel White taught twenty boys in his Classical and English School at 33 High Street; Mary Thompson, at No. 38, coached twenty-two pupils; farmer Pat Magill had a roll of thirty at No. 63, Church Street; and at No. 153, thirty-six studied with Jas. Wallace. The Kildare Society built two houses for education in the '3Rs'.

'There are few who cannot read; writing and arithmetic are not usually included in the female education but the majority of males can write. English grammar is now generally taught and the course of education has within a few years been greatly improved,' assessed the O.S. Memoir of the parish, 1838. A lending library opened in 1830 with 176 books and 16 subscribers. Literary and cultural societies began to flourish.

'Were we required to characterise this age of ours by any single epithet, we should be tempted to call it, not an Heroical, Devotional, Philosophical, or Moral Age, but, above all others, the Mechanical Age,' reflected Thomas Carlyle (1759–1881).

A 'four-wheeled caravan' offered the public transport to Ballymena at a cost of one shilling, in the 1830s. For an extra sixpence, one could travel to Belfast in the comparative luxury of a stage coach which left Ballymena at 4 a.m. and arrived in Antrim at 'the scrake of dawn'. An added delight was that the old route from Templepatrick via Craigarogan and Mallusk had, since 1832, been superseded by the 42 ft broad great Mail Coach and Turnpike Road (the present A6). Tolls at borough boundaries were abolished in 1857. And threepence could be saved on the two-hour Belfast journey by travelling on one of Antrim's three jaunting cars. Other connections were with Derry, Coleraine, Cookstown and Magherafelt. Tourists began arriving each summer on their way to Shane's Castle or the Giant's Causeway.

The Age of Machinery brought railway mania to Antrim in 1847. Single-span bridges were constructed at Muckamore and at the top of Fountain Street, and a bright, tidy station and goods yard appeared at the head of Station Road. The efficient little station had its own engine-driver, guard, gate-man, signalmen and ticket collector. But when station master, Andy McKillop, gave an incorrect order to one of his signalmen in 1876, the 'up' 10 a.m. passenger train met the 'down' goods train on the single line in the cutting at Moylena farm. Passengers were thrown on to the embankment by the impact, and Andy McKillop was thrown out of his job. (Margaret Irvine – a sister of Dr Alexander Irvine – was one of the casualties; there was at least one fatality).

A-HUNDRED-YEARS-AGO FOLK

Perhaps the most charming reminder of Old Antrim is the cast iron milestone at Castle Street which reassures the traveller – 'Antrim 0 Miles'; held by its charm, time's century-old veil moves aside . . .

. . . Two quiet, austere-looking magistrates descend the steps from the courthouse: J.P.s, Thomas Montgomery of Birch Hill and George F. Cavendish Clark of that elegant Regency style mansion 'The Steeple', built in 1827 beside the round tower. Clark's father, William, saved the tower from destruction in 1819.

> "George of the Steeple
> And Tom of Burchill –
> They do little good
> But they do little ill."

(Antrim street song)

Sing that and yilhafta run fur yerinfurit! And behind George and Tom troops yer man McTammany, solicitor's clerk, who 'goes along the streets jinglin' his keys and throwin' them in the air'.[88] You'd think he was affis bap!

There's a grand view from the courthouse steps. The bay windys and big hexagonal Italian tower with the spiral staircase on the castle's southern face were added in 1887. Across the square, beside the castle gate, stands the 1856 constabulary barracks, offices, yard and garden. Behind us, at No. 8 Market Square, beside the town's main water-pump, the first Ulster Bank was put up in 1865, though the original branch opened in August, 1836; the Belfast Savings Bank branch has been in business here since 1830.

All the streets were macadamized in the '30s, though the 'entries' were still either clabbery or cobbled. High Street is stikkinout for its fourteen grocers' shops, and twenty-two spirit dealers' premises. But the grandest establishments have to be Hall's (1897) First Class Family and Commercial Hotel (with 'private cars attending all trains'), the King's Arms (1754) but it has only four post horses, whereas there are eight stabled at the Massereene Arms, which hotel was headquarters for the military officers in that hot June of 1798! Rev. Dr Hannay, writing under the nom de plume of 'George Birmingham', sets part of his novel *The Northern Iron* in the same hotel. Thompson's (Antrim Arms) Hotel across the street has the largest dining room in town: seats one hundred! They run tours of the North (and the South) from Antrim. And then, of course, there's John Brotherton's Commercial Hotel.

'Lady cyclists are specially catered for,' they tell me, at Mrs Scott's High Street tea-rooms. The street's chief baker, Sam Johnson, is also the precentor of 1st Antrim Presb. Church; they say you can hear him a mile from the church when the windys are open in summer.

Barney McQuillan's master-cobbler shop, at the High Street – Bridge Street corner, is where you'd meet Willie Withero trudgin' home from his day's stone-breakin' at Killead. He comes up past Viscount Massereene's (1887) horseshoe-entrance blacksmith's forge. Beside Barney's, in the three-storey house, lives auld Mr Boyd. Of his three boys, Tom's manager of Greenmount's bleachgreens, Henry's joint-manager of Belfast's large hardware store of Riddel & Co., and John has just been promoted from Muckamore's 'Green' mill to manage Larne Harbour. Jane, Mr

Smithy, Antrim.

Massereene Forge.

Boyd's eldest girl, is matron of Antrim Workhouse, Lizzie has married Mr Stewart the schoolmaster, and the youngest daughter, Mary, will earn for herself an immortality as the 'cowerdy-custert' Miss Clarke Methodist tract distributor in the *Chimney Corner* book.

High Street's great hardware store belongs to the same William Vance who, when he was Chairman of the Town Commissioners in 1857, repaired and widened Massereene Bridge. Massereene itself is a fisherfolk's shanty hamlet: 'They pay little or no rent, own no land or boast not more than a little garden; break down the fences in the neighbourhood for fuel, trespass on the plantations for the same purpose, steal poultry and commit various petty depradations.'[20]

Auld Sammy Cooper, who keeps the general store beside the auld post office, is sexton of the parish church and when its clock strikes nine, Sammy'll be after tolling the evening curfew, . . . and so will fade the soft mellow light of paraffin oil lamps in homes where mothers can't be lion after 5 a.m. if they're to have the family and themselves out to work for sex in the mills in a manner of speaking. After the carl singers, Sammy goes a dinger a dozen times with the auld bell on the last night of every year, and then the Methodist preacherman gulders fernenst the parish church gates haranguin' the townsfolk: 'A few moments yet remain of the old year. You have yet time. This voice may never again warn you on a watch-night. Let your sinful life pass away with the old year – it is going, going, going – it is gone!'[88] Fernuf?

Notice the wee holes under the windys either side of All Saints' famous 1596 datestone (fronting Church Street)? Them's 'Leper Squints' from the days when undesirable characters were permitted only to have a 'keek' or squinty-view of proceedings inside the church.

Back in 1829, when Rev. J. Dawson Hull was curate of All Saints', he had a son born here – Edward – who is the famous Prof. Hull that's Director of the Geological Survey of Ireland and Professor of Geology at the Royal College of Science. Before his death (1917), Prof. Hull will win an international reputation as author of the ambitious *Sketch of Geological History, Being the Natural History of the Earth and its Pre-Human Inhabitants*.

Parish Church and Riverside, Antrim – Courtesy of J. P. Coyle.

Sammy Cooper's lad, William, is head bomadeer of thon wee drapery shop opposite the parish church, but isn't it cheek-by-jowl with those other drapers, Kennedy Hunter and little W. D. McManus!

After inspectin' the new (1869) south transept and robing room in All Saints', we could dawdle up Railway Street to sniff Sam Rea's flaxworks near the station, or dander down Riverside (Mill Row) to view the old House of Correction and the stocks, or the (1817) Union Dispensary and the old Celtic Paper Company Ltd., which is now a weavin' fectary. Or we could just stand aroun' and watch 'Jowler' Hainey and his wife competing against 'the fish woman' Eliza Wallace, sellin' pollans from Lough Neagh; 10d. a dozen. Then, forby, there's the 'Hern' (herring)-man, the Scissors-man, the Pack-man, the Fir-man, and Tom McGrath the Donkey (rag)-man.

With a hepney treacle half-bap from Sam Johnson's wife, Elizabeth, you'll hay the strength now to climb up the 'church street' we still call Scotch Quarter. The best homes here, braven offen, front on to the street. Away on your right is the abode of thon tall, portly solicitor chap, William Williamson. His sister lives opposite, not far below William Shannon's beside the (1806) Methodist church, just below the Kilyn Entry thonder.

The earliest known Methodist service held in Antrim was conducted in the courthouse in 1785 by none other than John Wesley hisself. Wesley came again, in 1787, to preach in the Unitarian church, and again, in 1789, when he was 86, which was just as well for a couple of years after that again he was dead. In 1816 the Methodists split into Wesleyans and Primitives, but they made up again in 1878. And then one of our Unitarians, Mary Mackey, split and made up with the Methodist preacher (William Johnston), and all because she took a fancy to their great singing at a local funeral. And didn't our new Mrs Johnston then go on to become the granny of Rev. Dr Crawford Johnston, founder of Belfast Central Mission.

Now you could sit on the roof of the Methodist Sunday School – and many's the lad has – and snip the apples from the trees (if you have a cattypult), in thon orchard of Wm. Shannon's brother (Graham), on t'other side of the church. Auld Graham

Pogue's Entry and 'Chimney Corner'.

Shannon loves for to sit footerin in his wee summerhouse in the corner of his fancy rose garden, and complain all the day about that one-eyed pub owner, Johnny Darragh, whose sons are forever hammerin' in the wee forge across the street. Though he was a cobbler wanst hisself, Shannon says all of the labourin' class in Antrim is right ijits and should stay tucked away down wunnathem narrow, cobbly 'entries' of the town; such as Williamson's, Darragh's, Adair's, Rooney's, Morwood's, Scott's, Dixon's, Ferguson's, Taggart's or Milliken's.

What yours truly likes best to see about them entries, for it's a relief to see it, is the hepney copy of the Belfast Tellygraph which they pass round the houses every night, not because the poor folk were wantin' to read, which they couldnay anyway, but because they was needin' lavatory paper!

'The Chimney Corner' interior of cottage.

Across from Graham Shannon's is where they call 'the bottom of the world': Adair's Entry, which, in times to come, will be mistakenly called Pogue's Entry! The chimney sweep, Billy O'Hare lives with his missus, Ann, in the more modern brickwork house on the left. See him? Sedsamarley! Himinhur live next door to that powerful fine rag-man, Tom McGrath (though he can be a bit coorse). Directly opposite McGrath, the rough-hewn Jamie Irvine runs his cobbler's shop in thon wee early-18th century labourer's cabin, just next door to Mary McConaghy.

Jamie's wuman, Anna, passed away on 12th July (and hur a Catholic!) 1889; and his sons – William, James, Alexander (Alec) and Dan – no longer bide here. Of the

Irvine girls – Margaret, Sarah, Elizabeth and Mary – only Mary (Scott) still lives in Antrim. You would say it's a grand family entirely. Their heroic fortitude and the manner in which not only the life of the family but of the immediate neighbourhood was coloured by the noble life and lips of the wuman who was Jamie's wife you'll find lovingly pictured in two of the best-loved and best-selling books by an Ulster writer: *My Lady of the Chimney Corner* and *The Souls of Poor Folk*, by Anna and Jamie's boy, Rev. Dr Alexander Irvine. Oh, and you might enjoy dippin' into *The Chimney Corner Revisited* as well, so you will.

Let's enter the Chimney Corner cottage as it is in the Irvines' time. Fernenst the wall on your right stands an old pine table which, at meal times, they take over near the fire. Above the table, nailed to the wall, is the shelf for their family 'china'. The second wall extends from the shelf to the chimney wall and in its centre is the door to the parents' bedroom. To the right of the door rests the wee ladder which serves as the staircase to the wee half-loft beneath the thatch where the childer sleep like spoons in a drawer.

Between the bedroom door and the chimney wall is a bench, and at its chimney end is the chimney corner where their ladyship spent her life. Did ever you see a corner so empty now she's gone? There's her salt-box hanging beside the stool she nailed into the corner. Many's the one about Antrim questions the 'saintliness' of Anna Irvine but sure they don't wear the love-tinted specs of her boy, Alec.

The wide hearth – you'll find no grate – is on a level with the mud flure and is paved with whitewashed cobble stones forby. Over the fireplace, old battered china ornaments, yellow with smoke of years, stand on the wide mantleshelf. There are no chairs; only creepie stools.

To the right of the windy is the visitors' corner where customers palaver on a long stool when Jamie works at his bench in front of the windy; by night, if he's no working by the light of thon large tallow candle in his threefut tall candlestick, he's sittin' there in a lonesome hush, smokin' his auld cutty pipe or rubbin' his auld nose till it starts to gleam.

Alexander Irvine (right) with
American novelist, Jack London.

Left of the windy hangs a powerful large wicker cage with 'Peter', the thrush, in it. Jamie made the cage hisself as he did the jamb wall beside the door to protect hisself from the draughts. By the way, the turf smoke in here'll choose the room instead of the chimney if the top half of the door isn't kept ajar.

From the roof hangs bunches of dried hoarhound and rosemary; useful for colds. The only 'pictures' on the whitewashed walls are poems which Anna has clipped from *The Weekly Budget* and framed between two pieces of glass, glued together with flour paste.

'Poverty', insists Alexander, 'inadequately describes the condition of life in that alley. It was stark destitution. We were all chronically, hopelessly hungry and utterly unconscious that there was anything unusual about it'; and we step outside to find the childer of the

Scott's Entry, Church Street.

neighbourhood scratching the offal in the dunghills and the gutterways! Bones sleeved in flesh.

In 1891, among the many, many hundreds of pounds left as benevolent funds by Mary Bruce's Will were £200 for the founding of Church Street's Bruce Memorial School and £100 for 'the deserving poor in the town or neighbourhood of Antrim irrespective of the religion of recipients'; another Lady of some chimney corner. And, sure, isn't there one in yur own family?

Pogue's Entry tunnel on to the street has us futtinit past the pig sty and under the house of the town's process server, fisslin John Conlon ('with his beaver slightly tilted to one side and his wellingtons which get in each other's way'[88]). His wife, Liza, was a tower of strength when Henry Leckey, the lough fisherman, was gayanbad. Liza made the shroud while Jane Burrows washed Henry's corpse and Margaret Houston comforted the grievin' mother, Eliza.

Next entry up, on this side, is Scott's; (used to be Rooney's). That's where Alec Irvine was born. Pop in? All up this side of Church Street there are cherry trees growin'; and isn't it no word of a lie they're all for us as a wee present from Henry Dupré Malkin Barton who lives at 'The Bush'. The big redbrick tower blocks with the huge Italianate clock tower up near Bush House are the new (1898) Holywell Hospital.

Rev. W. S. Smith.

Across Church Street now, of course, is the old Unitarian church and isn't the tall, three-storey skyscraper just above it its manse (No. 69), for the distinguished preacher and author, Rev. William Sunderland Smith (1833–1912). He was educated at the Unitarian Home Missionary College, Manchester, and held charges at Aberdeen, Doncaster and Crediton before spotting Antrim in 1872. Hasn't himself been President of the Unitarian Missionary Conference and President of the Non-Subscribing Presbyterian Association. Wasn't he married twice – Emma Grainger of Coseley, and Clara Ann Clark of Cirencester – and didn't he add three sons and two daughters to our population. Of course, he'll be best remembered for his writings about the '98 Rebellion, Shane's Castle, Lough Neagh and natural history; and his invaluable wee tome – *Historical Gleanings in Antrim and Neighbourhood* – published in 1888, might help some genius about a hundred years from now to piece together parts of the story of Antrim! Ah, will there ever be another Smith like him? Amno coddin.

'Castle Puff' we call Smith's manse. On occasions – Massereene 'occasions' – this imposing mansion was used to bed guests who were not quite elegant enough to qualify for residence at Antrim Castle, though they were sufficiently 'puffed-up' (in the opinion of the townsfolk) to lodge at Castle Puff! (Amawayon now . . .)

* * * * *

Church Street – Courtesy of Jackie Peacocke.

Talk about writers reminds the present writer of James Johnson who was born in Antrim in 1844. He became editor of the *Kingston News and Ottawa Citizen* in Ontario, Canada. After his death in 1905, his 'many Canadian and English friends' erected a handsome obelisk to his memory at the old graveyard, Muckamore. Beside it is a gigantic obelisk inscribed for 'they that go down to the sea in ships', with particular reference to our Antrim-born (1811) naval Captain William Kelly who died in 1877. Cpt. John Kelly, who was lost in a hurricane off Mauritius in 1866, is also honoured there, as are many Clotworthys, Molyneaux, Thompsons, Campbells, Morwoods, Byrnes, Dickeys and members of the Marquess families.

They do say that Antrim's the most literate of all the thirty-two counties, particularly between Antrim and Kells; no small factor in the birth of the 1859 Revival; remember, too, the Sixmilewater's 18th century 'rhyming weavers' – small farmers, country schoolmasters and handloom weavers – intoxicated wordsmiths rarely out of their depth when they hiked their way to that great lover of mankind (and womankind) by the banks o' bonie Doon.

Donegore churchyard, in the bare shadow of old Donegore Motte, is the grand resting place of Sir Samuel Ferguson; 'Ireland's greatest poet', according to William Butler Yeats. Ferguson was comfortably born into a Parkgate family descended from Scots-Cromwellians who had settled on an impressive chunk of Lough Neagh's Antrim shoreline which they had confiscated in the 17th century. Ironically, though Ferguson was a Tory, an Anglican and diehard Orangeman, the Celtic Twilight might never have dawned had it not been for Yeats' discovery of an obscure little lyric by Ferguson. The poem – *The Fairy Thorn* – was inspired by an Antrim tale about four young girls who were bewitched by the beauty and magic of fairy-folk when they stumbled upon a wee folks' dance. Yeats proclaimed Ferguson's poem as the inspiration of the literary birth of Ireland in his time. The Gaelic League, too, became strange fruit of Ferguson's attempts to glorify the Protestant Ascendancy as the true Irish, which he attempted to do by means of literary antiquarianism. With Ferguson's important discovery of the Cuchulainn and Red Branch Cycle, a ready-made romantic tradition was handed to Ireland, at a stroke. The final conquest of pre-Gaelic Ulster in 637 A.D. – recounted in Ferguson's mountainous epic, *Congal* (which goes on for ever!) – was stimulated by his scholarly translations of ancient manuscripts, deposited in his care as President of the Royal Irish Academy.

Though he longed to be remembered, this 'Homer of the Gael' lies forgotten among the Donegore brambles and the nettles and the Croppies of '98 below the cairns of an ancient civilisation; ancestral voices well-nigh forgotten nowadays. One can cast only a cold eye on the 1886 tombstone there which makes no mention that Sir Samuel Ferguson ever penned 'one word that waked'.

"Yet hold not lightly home, nor yet
The graves on Dunagore forget . . ."

from Westminster Abbey,
by Sir Samuel Ferguson.

Another memorial in that little churchyard, which conjures up weird, gruesome images is the low, substantial, gloomy-looking structure known as 'The Vault'. About it, W. S. Smith wrote in his *Ramble in Search of The Curious and Interesting (1883):* 'Before the requirements of medical schools were legally provided for, subjects for anatomical purposes were often procured in a surreptitious, sometimes in a murderous manner, and to prevent the graves in this burying-ground being desecrated and robbed, this building was erected for the reception of corpses. Here they were watched by anxious relatives until decomposition had rendered them futile for the objects for which they might be sought, when they were interred'. Antrim's Unitarian church has a similar 'bone house' in its burying-ground; (largely demolished in 1982).

Speaking of poets and W. S., the Rev. W. Bryson who lived in Castle Street's 'Frenchman's House' had a son – William A. – who was a bit of a poet until he met his premature waterloo in 1814 during a suicidal visit to the Six-Mile. Among his rhymes about battles and heroes, George 3 and the Irish, one refrain – 'On the banks of Moilena how oft have I strayed' – made W. S. Smith think Wully was 'doinaline', so the Rev. quipped: 'And what did the young poet stroll there for? To behold pleasant scenes – to contemplate the charming array of wood and water there met with? Oh dear, no; but to see his "beautiful maid", his "sensitive rose-bud".'

When Ossian – the famous warrior-poet and giant hallion of ancient sagas – fell in love, it was with that same rosy stretch of the Sixmilewater which sings through our parish, according to reports. Sadly, he forgot to pen anything which could be (even remotely) connected with our area! We press on up now to the Town-Head where lots of redbrick terraces have been built since 1870. One of the big houses belongs to James Prenter who became A.D.C. to the Prince of Wales and was with Lord Roberts in the famous 1880 march from Kabul to Kandahar.

Sir James Weir Hogg, Registrar of the Supreme Court of Calcutta and a director of the East India Company was born (1790) here. He declined seats offered in the Cabinets of Lord Melbourne and Sir Robert Peel!

And there's 'fat Hugh McGukin' waddling out of his house (opposite Prenter's), with his three wee dogs. He'll spend the best part of the day lolling against the GNR bridge blethering to John McConkey. Up here at the bridge you get a grand view down the town, and it looks even better when the lamp-lighter gets the street lamps to bathe the place in glory; there've been gas lights fizzing since 1855 and they do say they've got gas chandeliers in the castle. There's Dr A. Spearing in his gig taking his white beard and auld Dr Taggart away to Belfast for the day; that mail-coach-road cost £21,000 to lay in 1831 so that's why they put a toll-gate here.

And so we turn away from the main town and bid farewell to some of its more colourful characters: Hughie Thornton, the beggarman who wears two pairs of

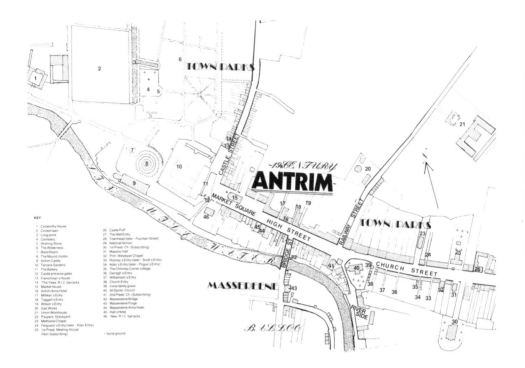

trousers and several waistcoats (all at the same time, the year round); huckster, Mary M'Donagh, with her wicker basketshop slung on her arm; and Felix Boyle, the bogman, with his auld rabbit-skin cap pulled down over his ears and the mare hauling along his cartful of turf.

Beyond the High Street ch. manse with its spacious orchards, above the railway bridge, there's a picturesque countryside of farms and snowy-white bleach greens – excepting the couple of cottages of Bob McCabe and Jas. Wray – until you come to Moylena's Quakers' graveyard (1701), next to Firgrove. Now there's far more than Reford family ghosts in the auld place; for instance, did you ever hear of Rev. Chas. H. Crookshank, the president of the Irish Methodist Conference held lately? His father, who wrote a *History of Methodism in Ireland* in Antrim, rests within among the Refords and along with his good wife and two daughters.

Ann's Hill, over the way, sees great celebrations every Easter Tuesday; a great occasion for music-making on the tin-whistle, fiddle and melodeon. The day before, about thirty couples form a circle down at the Fir Field and anyone asked for a kiss has to oblige. Quare fun's to be had running around the Fir Field with the one you fancy. The romantic sports day spills over into the Tuesdays at Ann's Hill, and the celebrations conclude with everyone – about a hundred and more – joining hands to form a human chain from one end of Antrim to the other; they call it 'threading the needle'. . . .

Oh for a wee country cottage and that knock on the kitchen door and a rhyming Jack Straw or Grand Turk claiming the privilege of Christmas in the admission of his merry-men. How often, these days, do St Patrick or Wee Divil Doubt or St George or Beelzebub still perform their seasonal rituals? The Rhymers – or Mummers – are mostly a ghostly memory now.

Gone too are the days of the big free slabs of fruit loaf and sweets at the Fir Field soirées when the Burnside Sunday School children would march down to join their Millrow brethren.

Antrim Hockey Club, 1912–13 – Courtesy of Louis Reford.

Massereene Golf Club.

Time was Christmas or Easter and the fairs were the only fun to be had, besides playing shinny or marbles. However, John Joseph Robinson, employed by York Street's Muckamore Mill, founded the grand Muckamore Cricket Club (first at Boghead and then at Harrigan's Hill behind Firgrove, in 1884); and twenty years later came the 'bully-off' for Antrim Hockey Club, opened one year before the inaugural tee-off for Massereene Golf Club. The latter's course is both exceedingly picturesque and valuable because its sandy loughshore location can attract many golfers from far-off and waterlogged fields. Ferrard Football Club was established in 1887.

The pre-1780 house at the junction of the Belfast and Oldstone roads is Moylena Cottage, home of His Majesty's Physician General in Ireland, William Chaine. His brother, John, was Dean of Connor, and another – James – was appointed Sherriff of Co. Antrim in 1873 and Westminster M.P. for the county ten years later.

James' grandfather shrewdly married into the Whittle family who helped set him up with a bleachworks of his own at Muckamore. His residence, like a castle on the Rhine, was Ballycraigy House. This William Chaine became Ireland's greatest bleaching magnate overnight, literally . . .

. . . One night, in 1823, Joseph Reford (grandson of the early 17th century Exeter bleacher invited to Antrim by the Clotworthys), was experiencing a small cash-flow problem and so fancied the prospect of winning at cards when William Chaine invited him up to Ballycraigy House. The story goes that Chaine planted a professional card player in the game and Joseph's inherited empire passed to Chaine at the turn of a playing card: bleachworks and greens, beetling mills, workers' homes, farms at Moylinny and Spring Farm, etc! Bankrupt, Joseph became an apprentice cabinetmaker in Antrim while Chaine rocketed to fabulous wealth. By mid-century, Chaine had bought over the Greenmount Thompsons' 'Muckamore Bleach Green with houses, mills, machinery, land, water-courses, weirs, dams, rights'. All of this and more (e.g. New Lodge, Summer Hill, Firgrove, Moylena Cottage, Boghead; even the Refords' Antrim Quaker Meeting-House), were willed through William's son, James (who married his cousin – a Whittle – from Castle Upton), to James the M.P.

James Chaine (1841–1885), operated Ballycraigy House as a palatial rival to the Massereenes' abode. Beside the tennis lawn were cages of prize golden pheasants. In the stables were fine hunter, carriage and racing horses; one regularly raced the Belfast train from Muckamore to Dunadry and another became a Derby winner. It was Willie Murphy, the head groom, who detailed young Alexander Irvine from Pogue's Entry to help the grooms, Willy Young and Charlie Austin. 'It meant something to be a horse in that stable', said Irvine; 'much more than it meant to be a groom!' But Alec Irvine turned out to be the only (teetotal) employee whom James Chaine would trust to escort a prize racer to the Chaine summer residence at Larne.

Having bought Larne Harbour for £20,000, Chaine revived the Larne-Stranraer connection. Larne, however, was the death of him for there, while bidding farewell to the Prince and Princess of Wales, he contracted pneumonia and was dead within the week. His dying wish was to be buried upright, in his full yachting gear, looking out to sea from the ancient Waterloo Fort earthwork on a hillside above Larne. The Chaine Memorial at the mouth of Larne Lough is an imitation of Antrim's round tower.

James died young but Joseph Reford's son, Robert (born at Moylinny Farm, 1831), emigrated and successfully founded the Robert Reford Shipping Company of Canada!

With the Canadian nephew (Mr Michael Reford) of the Company's late owner, the Author was intrigued to uncover (in a family tree successfuly traced back to Devon Wreyfords of 1440), direct descent (through a marriage) with Antrim's famous 18th century preacher, Rev. John Abernethy. (Among this family's many historic papers there is also mention of a Francis Comet Reford being born on 22 October, 1811 – Halley's Comet was apparently overhead at the time!)

Much remains of Chaine's properties: even his Ice House may still be found (in the railway tunnel opposite Muckamore Garden Village); 'New Lodge' is now farmed by Mr Wm. Clark. The sophisticated Ballycraigy House, alas, has been replaced with a housing estate shopping centre.

Some day they'll all just be names in a history book: Clark of the Steeple, Chaine (and later, Meenan) of Ballycraigy, Reford of Moylinny, Thompsons of Greenmount, Holmes of Holywell, McKeen of Loughanmore; the great and the near great, the wise and otherwise, the rich and the poor folk of old Victorian Antrim. And their distinctive houses? Most should survive the 20th century though some may only be guessed about – like the Montgomery's Birch Hill House (erected *c.* 1785 but destroyed by fire, November 1941, during U.S. military occupation), of which only the 1842 stables complex remains. Quaint little gatelodges, some still with their beautiful, leaded-windows, can still be found, in and around Antrim.

The County Council Act of 1898, which established elected county councils, marked the end of the grand juries which had given control over local government to the landlords.

A few miles further from Antrim, one may still admire the unostentatious Castle Upton at Templepatrick. Essex's Capt. Henry Upton married a daughter of Sir Hugh Clotworthy and their great-grandson – Clothworthy Upton – was elevated as 1st Baron Templeton in 1776. His son was created a viscount in 1806.

Knights of St John (Hospitallers) had a priory on this site from the 13th century until the Reformation. The monks took part in England's last Crusade, behind the

Castle Upton – Courtesy of Pat McGuigan.

banner of King Edward. (Tradition holds that St Patrick baptised converts at an ancient well in the village centre; c. 450 A.D.).

Today, however, one visits Castle Upton to admire the workmanship of the celebrated Robert Adam. He added two rooms, a grand staircase and imposing entrance hall in 1783. His north wing and stables were built in 1788; the latter are the most important surviving group of office buildings in Adam's Castle style. Edward Blore, who designed the embattled arched gateway at the village, restored the castle in 1837: principally, the north wing ballroom, the drawing room's oriel windows and the decorated library ceiling. The interested visitor will enjoy also the 'Norman' flanker towers which were added to the castle; all now the gracious home of Sir Robin and his artist – novelist wife, Lady Coralie Kinahan.

Adam's 1789 temple of death – Templeton Mausoleum – (adjacent to the castle), is one of the country's most perfect examples of European neo-classicism; a National Trust property. Though but a miniature version of the original design, this triumphal arch is also a beautiful sample of Adam's talent, notwithstanding that his work here was never completed.

THE TWENTIETH CENTURY

With the end of the Boer War on June 1, 1902, Antrim welcomed home its heroes: Lieut. John Weir West, C.B.E., C.M.G., K.H.S., Royal Army Corps; his younger brother, Frederick Buick West, Imperial Yeomanry; Wm. Gordon, 3rd Dragoon Guards; Robert Gordon, Joseph Young, James and Wm. Christie – all of the Imperial Yeomanry; James Scott, Diamond Fields Horse; and Alex Coleman, Baden-Powell's Mounted Police. 26 days later, Antrim enthusiastically celebrated King Edward 7's Coronation with a great bazaar.

Then came a new revolution: an agricultural one. Whereas formerly crop seed had always been scattered by hand, the new century saw seed sown and crops cut mechanically; 'and in the case of oats and wheat, not only cut', enthusiased one Antrim gent of the time, 'but bound up and cast aside mechanically, in readiness for stooking. It is really marvellous!' Where, once, cutting eight acres of wheat or oats

High Street, Antrim – Courtesy of Jackie Peacocke.

in a day could only be done by eighty men with shearing-hooks (sickles), now the same task was easily undertaken by a single binding machine and one attendant.

However, when fifty invitations were issued for an Antrim ploughing contest, in 1905, only seven enthusiasts turned up. These magnificent seven promptly formed the Antrim Agricultural Society and from their number elected John Kirk, J.P. (President), Robert Russell (Treasurer), T. K. Moore and James Morrison (joint-Secretaries); the other three became committee members. When they arranged a new ploughing event at Morrison's Crookedstone farm for February 14, 1905, four thousand people turned up to watch thirty-seven competitors.

The Society decided to hold a grand Agricultural Show at Mill Row on June 12. Lord Massereene agreed to be Patron to the Society. On that glorious June day a capacity crowd watched the opening ceremony, performed by J. S. F. M'Chance, J.P., Chairman of the County Antrim Agriculture Committee. As well as an encouraging entry of 204 horses and 120 cattle, there were sheep, pigs, poultry, eggs, butter and agricultural implements on show.

The Mill Row field proving too small to contain the event, Lord Massereene gave the Society a field beside the railway station to be a permanent site for the Society's shows from 1906; ('Antrim Show Grounds' is now a military headquarters).

The £1,000 six-hundred-seater grandstand erected in the exquisitely designed Show Grounds contributed greatly towards the success of the 1906 Show. Cash prizes to the tune of £240 and eleven silver challenge cups were awarded. To defray the great expenditure, the Society exercised their Midas touch between June 26-29, 1907, by transforming the Show Grounds with the carnival atmosphere of a great bazaar. Eight decades later, the Antrim (July) Agricultural Show remains a major event in the annual calendar of Antrim town and county.

According to the inscription on his tombstone (recently shattered), at the gate of Antrim's old Unitarian church, Captain James Fleming of the 16th New York Volunteer Cavalry 'was killed at Fairfax, Virginia, by a gang of Guerillas' in the year 1863. That was also the year of Alexander Irvine's birth in Antrim. And it was the year, too, when the 10th Viscount Massereene met with his fatal accident.

John Foster, 11th Viscount Massereene and Ferrard, like his father, was imbued

12th Viscount
Massereene & Ferrard (1912).

Jean Barbara Ainsworth,
Viscountess.

with a deep passion for music and was an accomplished violinist. He encouraged those in Antrim who possessed musical talents to form a private band at the castle in 1904; practising in peace in the purpose-built, circular 'Band Room' music-tower, on the eastern side of the castle; a property which had to be demolished after it was vandalised in our half of this century. Lord Massereene hired a professional London conductor and presented a set of brass and reed instruments.

The 11th Viscount once managed to upset Rev. Canon C. Moore, who protested (1889) to the Royal Historical & Architectural Association:

> In spite of all local remonstrance to the contrary, Lord Massereene had the tree in his park – planted by Cromwellian officers – cut down, and the very large stone which, it is said, John Wesley had used as a pulpit during a missionary tour in the neighbourhood, he removed and buried in the ground entirely out of spite, to serve as a foundation stone for one of the stays of a wire paling. One may well ask . . . Who will advocate the abolition of capital punishment while deeds like this are done?

The Gothic memorial to this Vis. M. & F., in the parish church, has an alabaster cartouche testifying to his interest in music, and alluding to his extension of Antrim Castle (1887), restoration of the parish church (1892), and erection of Massereene School (1904). (A mourning tablet in the church honours his son who, like his father, died in 1905.) Three years after Viscount John had married Florence, only daughter of novelist Mjr. George John Whyte-Melville, their second son was born who, in 1905, succeeded to the title as Lt Col Algernon William John Clotworthy Skeffington and Ferrard; 12th Viscount.

Born in Dublin (1873), and educated at Winchester and the Royal Military College, Sandhurst, the new Lord Massereene was serving with the 17th D.C.O. Lancers when his father's death occurred. During the South African War (1900–02) he had been wounded, twice mentioned in Dispatches, awarded the D.S.O. and Brevet Major. From 1907 he was a major of the North Irish Horse and a member of the National Defence Association. In 1914 he went with his regiment to France.

For his 1905 bride – Jean Barbara Ainsworth, elder daughter of Sir John Stirling

Ainsworth, Liberal M.P. for Argyllshire – he created Ferrard House (from English timber), opposite the Station Road vicarage of Rev. Maurice Henry Fitzgerald Collis, B.D.; a fellow Dubliner. London, however, invariably claimed possession of this lord and his lady during the 'London Season'. Fresh fruit and vegetables were received there from the gardens of Antrim Castle.

Their daughter, Lady Diana Skeffington, created a stir in Antrim when word was put around that she was a possible match for the then Prince of Wales – Edward, son of King George 5 and Queen Mary! Tragically, she died of a fever and no-one could save her, and that was the end of the beautiful Lady Diana swopping Antrim Castle for the Palace in London. While at her mother's home in Ardanaseig, Argyll, Lady Diana Elizabeth Margaret Skeffington contracted scarlatina. Her parents brought her to London where the young débutante succumbed to typhoid fever. She died on December 6, 1930, and was interred in the grounds of Antrim Castle.

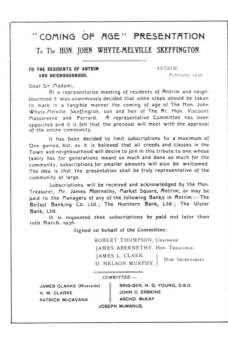

Prince Edward became (the uncrowned) King Edward 8 and was later forced into abdication and retirement as the Duke of Windsor, husband of Mrs Wallis Simpson. In 1981, another Lady Diana (Spencer) married another Prince (Charles) of Wales. And in 1732, a Lady Diana (Spencer) had refused the offer of marriage from HRH The Prince of Wales. What if the young and beautiful Lady Diana S. from Antrim had lived?

Viscount Massereene returned to Antrim after the war. He continued his father's sponsorship of the Massereene Brass and Reed Band; apparently musical talent was a prerequisite for employment within Antrim Castle. 'To revive and stimulate a love for music in our ancient town', declared the Viscount, and to raise funds to replace instruments, a grand bazaar was held in the Castle Grounds in June 1912. He took particular pride in showing the guests the spectacular Mexican pine (which annually provides us with giant cones); a gift from Sir John Ross of Rostrevor (whose ancestor not only captured Washington in the 1814 American War but also burned the White House).

Massereene personally planted the magnificent (and now mature) willow trees which grace the (Forum's) banks of the Sixmilewater; hoping to provide posterity with a plentiful source material for the making of cricket bats. The large green (between the Castle Farm and the long double lakes), was laid out as a cricket green. And all around, rare tree species of prime quality were planted – the redwood, blue fir, etc. – and which have matured magnificently for us to appreciate, even though many were planted too closely together – to 'fill a space' – and some were damaged in the fierce winter storm of 1983.

On 28th October, 1922, a Grand Ball was arranged at Antrim Castle. Parties at the castle generally cost around £2,000; a princely sum. It was a fateful night.

Somehow the grand staircase in the entrance hall caught fire. As the fire rapidly spread through the rectangular, box-like building, orders were issued that the water-storage tanks in the attic should be punctured. Curiously, these tanks – which ought to have been filled to capacity, particularly on the evening of any function in the

Antrim Castle Ruins – Courtesy of Z. Montgomery.

building – were discovered to be empty! The servant, whose job it was to ensure the tanks were kept well supplied, was also discovered to be missing, along with his suitcases; and was later reputed to be a Sinn Feiner.

With Belfast's fire brigade preoccupied that night with three city fires, guests, servants and townsfolk manhandled buckets of water from the river; others rushed through the twenty-yard tunnel at the 'Sunken Garden' to operate the double-handed pump there which drew water from the long double lakes in the grounds to supply the attic tanks. But the historic castle burned uncontrollably.

Gutting the building, the blaze consumed priceless historic paintings, books, parchments and furnishings, including the Oak Room's treasured Speaker's Chair from the Irish Parliament. (Much was looted the following morning.)

To the horror of everyone assembled before the blazing castle, a figure was spied at an upper window: one of the servants – 22 year old Miss Ethel Gilligan, of Castlepollard, Westmeath – was still trapped in her room. Townsman, Sam Hannan – a veteran and hero of Thiepval during the Great War – rushed a ladder to her window and carried the severely burned girl to the lawn below; though she died of her injuries, Sam's bravery was recognised with a parchment from the Royal Humane Society.

The historic Castle of Antrim stood in ruins. A claim for £90,000 compensation was lodged in 1923 for the castle and its contents. Certainly Shane's Castle had been burned by Sinn Feiners but arson at Antrim Castle could not be proved. Judge Thompson, Recorder of Belfast, disallowed the Antrim claim, ruling that the fire could have begun accidentally; an appeal against that judgment also failed.

Thereafter the gaunt ruins and its estate were said to be haunted by Ethel Gilligan's ghost and, following Lord Massereene's death (1956) in Clotworthy House, the ghost of his late lordship. Following reports of two white apparitions swooping down with wailful mourning calls on even the most sceptically intelligent of evening visitors to the Castle Grounds, Antrim R.U.C. mounted an official 'ghost watch' in the late 1960s. The officers were rewarded with the spectacle of a visitation by two large and ghostly-white shapes descending upon them from the charred ruins of the castle: two large, white owls!

THE LORDS OF MASSEREENE

1. **SIR HUGH DeCLOTWORTHY** (m. Marion Langford), d. 1630.
2. **SIR JOHN CLOTWORTHY** (m. Margaret Jones-Ranelagh), 1st Viscount Massereene, d. 1665.
3. **SIR JOHN SKEFFINGTON** (m. Mary Clotworthy), 2nd Viscount Massereene, d. 1695.
4. **COL. CLOTWORTHY SKEFFINGTON** (m. Rachel Hungerford), 3rd Viscount Massereene, d. 1713.
5. **SIR CLOTWORTHY SKEFFINGTON** (m. Catherine Chichester), 4th Viscount Massereene, d. 1738.
6. **SIR CLOTWORTHY SKEFFINGTON** (m. i. Ann Daniel; ii. Elizabeth Eyre), 5th Viscount Massereene, 1st Earl of Massereene, d. 1757.
7. **CLOTWORTHY SKEFFINGTON** (m. i. Mme. Marie Annettee Barcier; ii. Elizabeth Blackburn), 6th Viscount Massereene, 2nd Earl of Massereene, d. 1805.
8. **COL. LORD HENRY SKEFFINGTON** (unmarried), 7th Viscount Massereene, 3rd Earl of Massereene, d. 1811.
9. **LORD HENRY CHICHESTER SKEFFINGTON** (m. Harriett Jocelyn), 8th Viscount Massereene, 4th Earl of Massereene, d. 1816.
10. **RT HON. THOMAS HENRY FOSTER** (m. Harriett Skeffington), 9th Viscount Massereene, 2nd Viscount Ferrard, d. 1843.
11. **JOHN FOSTER** (m. Olivia O'Grady), 10th Viscount Massereene, 3rd Viscount Ferrard, d. 1863.
12. **JOHN FOSTER** (m. Florence Whyte-Melville), 11th Viscount Massereene, 4th Viscount Ferrard, d. 1905.
13. **LT COL. ALGERNON WILLIAM JOHN CLOTWORTHY SKEFFINGTON** (m. i. 1905: Jean Barbara Ainsworth; ii. 1940: Ms Florence C. Vere-Laurie), 12th Viscount Massereene, 5th Viscount Ferrard, d. 1956.
14. **JOHN CLOTWORTHY TALBOT FOSTER WHYTE-MELVILLE SKEFFINGTON** (m. Annabelle Kathleen nee McNamara Lewis, of Combwell Priory, Kent), 13th Viscount Massereene, 6th Viscount Ferrard, b. 1914.

Heir: John David Clotworthy Whyte-Melville Foster Skeffington; m. Ann Denise née Rowlandson; (elder son: Charles John Foster Clotworthy Whyte-Melville Skeffington).

The 12th Viscount was the first Parliamentary Secretary to Northern Ireland's first Prime Minister, Lord Craigavon, and was a Senator for eight years from his election in June, 1921. Then he removed to England though, in 1947, he decided to return to Antrim, take up permanent residence at Clotworthy House and to actively interest himself again in public affairs. During the '30s and '40s he'd often visited Antrim, particularly whenever the syndicate of gentlemen met for the traditional pheasant shoot. The hotel we call the 'Deerpark' was built by Massereene as a shooting lodge.

Staff were still employed in the Castle Grounds, particularly to breed and rear pheasants; 'cost £1 to rear one o' them there birds and a 2d. cartridge to put paid to it', an old retainer informed the Author; 'In them days, in the Castle Grounds, either you were trippin' over rabbits – scores o' them – or gettin' hit up the face with one of them there birds suddenly flappin' up at you.'

Lord Massereene expressed deep satisfaction that Clotworthy House was well tended: 'I like the way they keep it smart; kept in best military fashion'. He hoped it would always continue to be of use to the people of Antrim. Prophetic thoughts.

After the death of the Viscountess in 1937, his lordship married Mrs Florence Clementine Vere-Laurie, of Carlton Hall, Notts, the eldest daughter of the Hon. Sydney Foster-Skeffington, third son of the 10th Viscount Massereene. Her first husband was killed in action with the Royal Irish Rifles in 1915.

To the memory of these Massereenes, twin Celtic Cross monuments still stand in the Castle Grounds' little private cemetery where his lordship had buried his daughter, Diana, and, in 1919, erected Baron Oriel's memorial urn to Viscountess Margaretta, which had been brought from Oriel Temple. An unusual entrance to the cemetery was formed by using two giant stone acorns (which remain today) to support two arching whalebones, each nine feet in length.

After the 12th Viscount's death in 1956, Clotworthy House, for thirteen years, served as residence for Canon Collis and his wife. The complex was renovated for them and made habitable by their son – a famous surgeon whose expertise is remembered in the 'Colles Fracture' term for the 'dinner-fork deformity' produced by a displacement of the lower end of the radius (and usually accompanied by a fracture of the styloid process of the ulna).

The 13th Viscount of Massereene (and 6th of Ferrard), is that most worthy and pleasant and noble man, John Clotworthy Talbot Foster Whyte-Melville Skeffington, who married a daughter of S. African mining magnate, Henry Lewis. Son and heir is the Hon. John David Clotworthy Whyte-Melville Foster Skeffington; b. 1940. The family seat is now Chilham Castle, Canterbury, elegantly situated in grounds landscaped by Capability Brown. (Much may still be learned about the Clotworthys and Uptons by visiting Moneymore's National Trust property, Springhill House.)

Antrim Castle wore its death mask for almost half of the 20th century before being finally bulldozed. The 1887 hexagonal Italian tower remains, overlooking the terraces. Fortunately, however, the oldest and historically most important feature of the castle – the elaborate Jacobean cut-stone armorial bearings which graced the east front – still survives.

On this slab, the family arms, mottoes and events of history connected with the family are sculpted. At the top is the carved head of Charles 1, with Royal letters underneath; 'C' on one side of the crown and 'R' on the other. Below these are two shields, one with the arms of Sir Hugh Clotworthy and the other of his wife, Mary Langford, with the date between them. On the dexter, 'Castrum hoc cond'; in the centre, 'Decimo maii'; on the sinister, 'Anno domino, 1613'; and under the initials, 'H. C.' and 'M. C.' Below these initials is the inscription, 'Reno c. comes Massereene, MDCCIII', which was placed there by Chichester, 4th Earl of Massereene. Following the inscription are the arms of Clotworthy, 4th Viscount Massereene, with those of Chichester impaled. Still lower is the following inscription on a circular slab: 'HOC CASTELLUM AUSPICE JOANNE CLOTWORTHY UNDECIMO VICE COMITE MASSEREENE REFECTUM ET AMPLIFICATUM EST A.D. MDCCCLXXXIX'.

Hopefully, to complement Lady Marian's wolfhound statue, the armorial bearings will be re-erected someday in the Castle Grounds (or other public but vandal-proof location).

Among the four grandchildren of Sam Cody and his wife (who emigrated from Antrim to N. America in the 18th century), was Samuel Franklin Cody: Texan cowboy, bronco-buster, frontiersman, circus sharp-shooter, horse racer, showman, barnstormer, man-carrying kite inventor and pioneer British aviator. When this Indian-fighting, poker-playing son of America's Wild West came to Britain, he invented for the War Office a kite capable of carrying a soldier over enemy positions. It wasn't long before this trail being blazed by S. F. Cody was to lead to Antrim's old Deer Park; a launch pad for the history of British aviation.

Just a half dozen years after the Wright Brothers made man's first successful flight in a heavier-than-air machine, Henry George (Harry) Ferguson became the first Briton to build and fly his own aircraft. After a 130 yds trial lift-off at Hillsborough, Harry Ferguson made his first truly successful flight from Antrim Castle's Deer Park (April, 1910), in his famous 35 h.p. 8-cylinder JAP engine aeroplane. (In the same district, just five miles from Antrim town, the Province's first aerodrome – Aldergrove – was constructed, before the end of the 1st World War. By May 1983, the world's fastest and most famous jetliner, 'Speedbird 74 PAPA' – 'Concorde' – was soaring 35,000 feet into the heavens above Antrim, commuting to Paris, at about 1,350 m.p.h. – twice the speed of sound!)

The War Office requisitioned Antrim Workhouse in 1914 as a military barrack and store; the Workhouse office-building remained the headquarters of Antrim Rural District Council. 1,050 inmates had crowded the Workhouse back in 1846 but by 1912 only 121 occupied the complex and by 1914 the number had dropped to just 111. With an outbreak of diphtheria in 1915, however, the War Office returned the fever hospital for local use and the Workhouse was derequisitioned in August, 1916.

Greenmount estate (purchased in 1910 by the Department of Agriculture and opened in 1912 with eleven students as an agricultural college), Birch Hill House and 'Castle Puff' were also requisitioned. The YMCA camp at Antrim Showgrounds and the Castle Grounds also served as military quarters. The Government reputedly spent £200,000 providing accommodation in Shane's Castle estate for some nine or ten thousand sick or wounded soldiers invalided back from the trenches.

For the lads of Antrim who perished, official war graves were provided in the town's Moylena Road cemetery: Private T. Dunlop, Royal Inniskilling Fus., d. 26/1/15; Cpt. John Kirk Boal, 1st Batt. Royal Irish Fusiliers, killed in action (aged 20) at Rouex, France, 3/5/17; Thomas Henry Christie, killed in action (aged 25), 16/8/17; David McGrath, Canadian Infantry Bn., missing at Vimy Ridge, 1917; J. Coleman Kirk, 49th Batt. Canadians, killed in action at Inchy, near Cambrai, 27/9/18; and Private J. Crilly, Royal Irish Fusiliers, 22/5/19.

Among the many who never returned was Somme hero Lt Ezekiel Vance, who died of wounds in a German hospital at Candrey, 15/7/16; a grandson of the celebrated Ezekiel Vance, the 1798 hero of Antrim.

'After the war everything seemed in a flourishing way,' noted Antrim minister, Rev. M. Majury; 'The young men had returned home and the disillusionment of war had not begun.' Lest anyone should forget, however, two Great War cannons were set in concrete mounts beside the 'fountains' (water pumps) at Fountain Street and at the Court House.

Inglis & Co. carts trundled through the town every day bringing fresh English muffins, Scotch bannocks, oatcakes and delicious swiss rolls. A Sun Laundry van arrived from Larne every Wednesday advising the citizens that the Laundry 'is situated at the seaside and has an inexhaustible supply of pure water well adapted for washing purposes'. M. & A. H. Frew were High Street's leading milliners, costumiers and general drapers, guaranteeing 'perfect fitting'. Everywhere, shop windows were bright with their oil or gas lights. Souvenirs of Antrim in Irish marble

1st World War YMCA Camp, Antrim Show Grounds.

or Irish bog oak could be purchased from jeweller, J. Murphy. W. T. Lowry was also a jeweller and watchmaker as well as being the agent for the White Star, Anchor, Allan, Orient and S. African lines; Imperial and Meteor Rovers, Royal Enfield and Humber cycles. At D. & R. Barr's Cycle Depot a 'standard cycle' would cost ten guineas but for that you also got 'a free wheel and two rim brakes'.

'Airborne' bikes became an annual attraction, from 1922 onwards, at the Ulster Grand Prix circuit. Antrim emptied for the event as Charlie Dodson, Tyrell Smith, Graham Walker or Joe Craig swung round 'The Green' corner, at Muckamore, to disappear in the direction of Lylehill at a record-breaking 72 m.p.h.

Former staff officer of 108th Infantry Brigade, Ulster Division, Major G. F. Cavendish-Clarke, in 1927, put the famous Round Tower on the 'for sale' market, together with his 'Steeple' residence: '4 reception rooms, 7 bedrooms, 2 bathrooms and closet; ample culinary and servants' apartments; central heating, electric light, garage and stabling'. The successful bidder was Mr Samuel Fawcett, the proprietor of the Antrim Arms Hotel. (Today, the Northern Bank occupies the site where the Antrim Arms was razed by fire. Fawcett also owned 'Northlands', at the top of Fountain Street; the property later passed into the ownership of Catherwoods which family has given the modern age an important national figure in Sir Frederick Catherwood, H.R.C.)

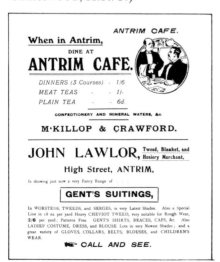
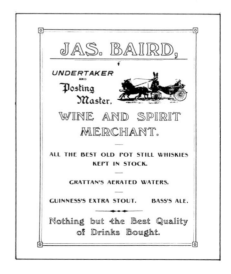

FAWCETT'S ANTRIM ARMS HOTEL, ANTRIM
HEADQUARTERS OF FAWCETT'S HOLIDAY TOURS, PARTY OF
TOURISTS LEAVING HOTEL FOR DAILY TOUR.

Courtesy of Jackie Peacocke.

Great Northern Railway (Ireland).

EXCURSIONS AND TOURS
From Antrim.

SUMMER SEASON.

To	1st Class	2nd Class	3rd Class	
Warrenpoint	15/3	10/-	6/6	Issued on Saturdays, available for return up to and including following Mond'y
Do.	15/9	11/9	8/9	Issued Daily, available for Return within two months
Newcastle, Day Trip on Wednesdays by 10-10 a.m. Train	5/-	3/6	2/6	Available day of issue
Do.	10/6	7/9	5/3	Issued on Saturdays, available for return up to and including following Mond'y
Do.	13/-	9/9	7/-	Issued Daily, available for Return within two months
Bundoran	28/-	22/9	17/-	Issued Daily, available for Return within two months

Cheap Tickets, available for day of issue only, are issued from **ANTRIM** to **BELFAST**, on Wednesdays by the following trains :—

	RETURN FARES.		
	1st Class	2nd Class	3rd Class
7-55 a.m. and **10-10** a.m.	3/-	2/5	1/6
Saturday to Monday Fares Antrim and Belfast	3/9	3/1	1/11

	SINGLE			RETURN		
	1st Cl.	2nd Cl.	3rd Cl.	1st Cl.	2nd Cl.	3rd Cl.
Ordinary Fares Antrim and Belfast,	3/-	2/5	1/6	5/-	4/-	2/6
Combined Rail and Cycle Tickets, by Afternoon Trains, Antrim & Belfast	3/-	2/5	1/6			

For further particulars, please see the Company's Tourist Programme.

JOHN BAGWELL, General Manager.

1912

Hotel business flourished with tourists from home and abroad alighting from the trains or privately-owned buses (such as Wright's Safety Coaches), at the county town advertised as the gateway to '160 miles of the finest coast scenery in the world, with a climate that God made for holidays'. Fawcett's charabancs at the Antrim Arms offered tours from Dunluce to the Mountains of Mourne.

'During the summer over 6,000 tourists have been catered for, and this figure will increase year by year,' announced W. T. Cooper, Chairman of Antrim Town Commissioners, on the occasion of the official switching-on of the town's new electric lighting system, in the autumn of 1929. 'Antrim is a progressive town,' he continued, 'and it is up to us to make it attractive.'

One of the Town Commissioners, who had been chairman in 1924, was Charles Burrowes. His 'Antique Galleries', in the old Unitarian Manse, housed one of Britain's finest collections. A native of Antrim, he was churchwarden of All Saints' Parish Church for many years and an enthusiastic playing member of the old Antrim Cricket Club. Always a staunch Unionist of the old school, he took a deep interest in public affairs.

But it was the Bishop of Kilmore, the Rt Rev. Dr Barton, D.D., of 'The Bush', Antrim, who put up the sale of the century: the Emperor Napoleon's Chair, brought here by Sergeant James Graham, who had slammed closed the gates of Hougoumont at Waterloo, in the face of the French army. The Bishop sold it to Louis Tussaud's Exhibition in July, 1934, for £190. (Fifty years later, however, Antrim is still the

84

Armistice Day, 1934, Antrim. Mrs N. Kirk and her Poppy Day Girls
and Drivers – Courtesy of Jackie Peacocke.

home for the chair of Gen. Gordon of Khartoum!)

In Castle Street, during the '30s, Mrs O'Connor operated a confectionery shop and there was a ladies' outfitter run by Eva Crawford. Nearby, in Market Square, James Abernethy managed W. D. McManus' outfitters for ladies, gents and children. In the Square and High Street, Sam Anketell had taken over R. Anderson's grocery business. Stephen Sloan, butcher, and Mrs Simpson's bookselling and stationery business were set fair for many more years trading; both in High Street, Simpson's being located at the premises recently vacated by Eason's.

Church Street seemed dominated by outfitters: William Dougall's, John Lawlor's and Wright's. Among them were the confectionery shops of Mrs R. Brown and, at No. 4, James Carson, who was also a fruiterer. Mrs Nicholl's shop at No. 21, as the sign above the shop window tells us, was 'established 1924'. Miss A. Mackey sold confectionery and light groceries from her shop at Fountain Street; a street 'famous' for such grocers as William French, Robert McCrory and Thomas Swann. Samuel Rea's Steam Saw and Turning Mills operated near the railway station, while David Rea's Antrim Saw Mills operated at Castle Street. Dentist, optician and distinguished Town Commissioner, Frederick T. Smith, J.P., was establishing such a chemist's shop that, even in the 1980s, 'Smiths Chemists' would occupy the central position in Antrim's ultra-modern central shopping complex. What changes there have been since the days of Smith's Medical Hall, the Town Farm behind it and Adair's Temperance Hotel!

Half a century ago, if you wanted any coal you simply phoned 65 for David Rea or 9 for Samuel Rea. Dialling Antrim 30 brought James Baird on the line to arrange your booking of either his 'wedding carriage' or 'horse hearse'. At the turn of this century, it was 'Blair & Baird' who made rejoicing or grieving a speciality. James 'Baird's Hotel' in Church Street had stabling accommodation for 40 horses.

Rev. Canon Collis, Vicar of Antrim, dedicating the stone erected as a memorial to Alexander Irvine's Lady of the Chimney Corner – his mother, Anna – and Jamie, his father; Antrim Parish Church, 27th October 1927.

Dr Alexander Irvine and his sister Mary (Scott), in The Chimney Corner, Pogue's Entry.

'The art of the town was centred in the church,' observed Alexander Irvine, 'and apart from the church services, the church itself had a refining influence.' Many fine memorials in the Moylena Road town cemetery testify to the greatness of the principal clergy of the time. There rest W. S. Smith (d. 1912), for 40 years Minister of the old Unitarian congregation; Rev. John H. Orr, Minister of High Street Pres. Church for 44 years, and one-time Clerk of the General Assembly (d. 1895); Rev. W. A. Adam, Minister of Orr's congregation for 32 years (d. 1927); Rev. D. H. Craig (d. 1945) of 2nd Donegore, and Rev. Alexander McKinney (d. 1934) of 1st Donegore; Rev. M. H. F. Collis, Vicar of Antrim (1890–1945) and Dean of Connor for 14 years (d. 1947), who rests with his two wives (Constance Mary, d. 1902; Ida Kathleen, d. 1964), and his youngest daughter, Frances; and, of course, Henry Dupré Malkin Barton of 'The Bush'.

The Rev. Thomas West, D.D., rests beside 1st Antrim church where he ministered for over 53 years. He was greatly respected throughout Antrim – Chaplain of Antrim Union, President of Antrim Literary Society, Chairman of the School Attendance Committee and manager of seven national schools – and nominated Moderator by the Pres. General Assembly in 1916. He married Helen Buick, daughter of Rev. F. Buick, Trinity Church, Ahoghill.

On 29th September, 1934, Church Street was thronged with crowds from home and abroad. From a platform erected on the street in front of Pogue's Entry, Viscount Massereene and Ferrard chaired the official dedication of the Chimney Corner cottage 'that this humble dwelling may be kept intact and unspoiled by time or circumstance, to bear silent and eloquent witness to the great love that dwelt there, and to the affection and reverence that a son of Antrim has for his mother'.

Pogue's Entry had become famous the world over, since 1913, as the setting for Dr Alexander Irvine's best-seller *My Lady of the Chimney Corner*, and its sequel *The Souls of Poor Folk*, published in 1921. Dr Irvine had achieved fame as the writer of many other books and articles too, as the minister of 'the millionaire's church' on New York's Fifth Avenue and as a romantic socialist visionary. He had been presented to kings, undertaken assignments from (the American and Mexican) Presidents and the British Prime Minister. During World War 1 he was the chief morale officer of the Allies at the Front. Among his friends he could count Jack London, George 'AE' Russell, Einstein, Madame Curie, Mark Twain, O'Henry and J. M. Barrie. His own incredible life story would fill a book or six.

> "I come back to Antrim the most astounded man in creation. I was thoroughly unconscious of any prospect that *My Lady of the Chimney Corner* would be so widely read. I though that perhaps my sister, Mary, would read it and I sent her a copy. But Ulster has recognised it more than any place."
>
> Dr Alexander Irvine

Following Dean M. H. F. Collis' dedication, the ceremonial opening of the celebrated cottage, the presentation of an (Old-Master?) oil painting by Jean Francois Millet and signings of the visitors' book, Alex and Mary laid a wreath at the parish church memorial (provided in 1927 by public subscription from the people of Belfast) to their humble parents. More than a half-century later, the same visitors' book receives fresh signatures, almost every day, with addresses from North America to South Australia! 'How curious,' observed Dr Irvine, 'that although many rich and noble people have been buried at All Saints' during the centuries, only the graves of a cobbler and his wife draw all sorts and conditions of people to that old graveyard.' (More than a century ago, it was estimated that over 8,000 people had been buried in this churchyard!)

Dean Collis' (second) wife – Ida Kathleen Collis – nurtured the Antrim Girls Friendly Society, assisted with the staging of their several operettas and John Entwistle conducted the small orchestra. On each of the five occasions when Ms. Dorothy Clarke entered her choir in the Belfast musical competitions they took first place and were welcomed home with a turn-out of the Massereene Brass and Reed Band (then based in their Castle Street Band Room hut).

The beginning of the end of the old Antrim so well known to our grandparents came, perhaps, in the spring of 1938 with the fire which destroyed Sam Fawcett's Antrim Arms Hotel. But there were darker clouds looming than the ones of smoke which billowed from the old hotel.

The outbreak of war created many difficulties. With conditions at a low ebb, at Old Bleach (Randalstown) for example, redundant clerical workers and warehousemen with years of experience in the linen industry easily found ready employment at Aldergrove. 'Sure, it was the making of "23MU" (RAF),' I'm told, for such work, apparently, was 'only fun for them!'

Within hours of war being declared on 3 September, 1939, Antrim lost a daughter of the late James and Jane Coleman (York Lodge): Helen West Burrows, a passenger aboard the 15,000 ton British liner *Athenia*, which was torpedoed and sunk by a German submarine. To Moylena Road's war graves were added ones for LAC Gerald McElrea, killed by enemy action, 1940; Lieut. William Jameson, R.N.V.R., lost at sea on active service, 1942; RAF Flight Engineer, James Bell, killed on active service, 1944; and Squadron Leader, C. J. F. Macrea, RAF, killed in action, January 1945. (Also killed in action were, from Shane's Castle, Brian Arthur O'Neill [1940] Captain, Irish Guards, and Shane Edward Robert O'Neill [1944] 3rd Baron O'Neill, Lt.-Col., North Irish Horse.)

British, American, Belgian and Dutch army bases were set up at the Castle Grounds, Lough Road, Shane's Castle, Ballycraigy 'Castle', Greenmount; around the district too, as at the old Dunadry mill, for example. The YMCA operated a fine canteen in Castle Street while the American Red Cross had another in Railway Street. The Show Grounds, beside the railway station, were transformed into a prisoner-of-war camp. The Admiralty tested torpedoes from the platform they constructed (which remains) in the lough.

Langford Lodge, just south of Muckamore (and now the location of an internationally-important aircraft-ejector-seat testing company), became 'Station 597': the United States Air Force' principal European repair depot, operated by the Lockheed Overseas Corporation. Also located on the base were No. 22 Veterinary Section; Nos. 897 and 1145 Military Police Companies; No. 401 Signal Company and No. 402 Station Gas Defence Detachment. Continuous harrassment of the enemy was made possible by flying out from this area (and others) combat crew replacements for lost crews operating from British mainland bases. Glenn Miller played two concerts at Langford Lodge in August, 1944.

When 20,000 USAAF servicemen took over the RAF's defence of Northern Ireland, the historic estates of the Langfords, Clotworthys and O'Neills about Lough Neagh became a vast assembly and training ground for the Allied invasions of Europe and North Africa.

On a sorry note, however, racial tension between white and coloured USA servicemen was so volatile that one of their number was brutally murdered close to Massereene Bridge.

With the Allies on the defensive by June, 1944, Antrim's vital war role was at an end. (Forty years on, the Northern Ireland Airport Authority would again offer the American Government a staging facility for US military aircraft, at Belfast International Airport, just outside Antrim.)

Building materials being scarce, during and after the war, restrictions prohibited the construction of private houses costing more than £100. Two estates, complying with the restrictions, were erected: one (since demolished) at Randalstown Road, opposite the Royal Engineers' complex; and Riverside's Belmont Park prefabricated dwellings. Mainly of aluminium construction, Belmont Park was expected to have a life of ten years but has survived to the present day.

On Saturday, 27th July, 1946, Rev. Robert Craig (Ballymena), Rev. William Mitchell (Antrim) and the Vicar of Antrim, Rev. S. P. Kerr received at Pogue's Entry the ashes of the late Dr Alexander Irvine who had passed away at Los Angeles in 1941. Four nephews – Thomas, William and Alexander Scott and Henry Adams – carried the plain bronze casket to the parish church. The memorial address was delivered by the Lord Bishop of Down and Dromore as Alexander was laid in his parents' *Love is Enough* grave in the picturesque old parish churchyard.

Shortly before James Chaine's death, the York Street Flax Spinning Co. Ltd acquired much of its power by purchasing much of his Muckamore mills, bleach-greens and watercourses. With the purchase of White's Flour Mill (formerly Whittle's Corn Mill), and the construction of the Islandbawn-Muckamore railway siding to supply coal for the new steam engines at the mills, York Street had an expanding complex at Muckamore, under the management of Ferguson Grainger.

(An excellent study of two hundred years of linen manufacture in the Antrim area, *Weaving Webs of Wealth* has recently been published by Ms. Heather Thompson.)

Lamonts continue the linen tradition in the Boal's old Riverside weaving factory (former paper mill), which they purchased in 1921. By the middle of the 20th century, however, the manufacture of synthetic fibres effectively silenced the mills of the Sixmilewater. York Street opted for voluntary liquidation (1961), demolition crews erased the village of Bog Head and nature began colonising industrial ruins.

British Enkalon PLC – Courtesy of British Enkalon.

THE NEW PLANTATION

It's no ill wind that sweeps across Lough Neagh from the south-west most of the year round, though yachtsmen who know that it is one of the world's roughest lakes may not agree. However, south-westerlies prevailing across the lough's 400 sq. km. bless Antrim with the rare treasure of an uncontaminated atmosphere. Mild winters are enjoyed and there is relatively little snow, fog or thunder. Light refracted over the great lough often paints the evening skies about Antrim with sensational sunsets.

A plentiful supply of water and a pollution-free atmosphere favoured Antrim, in 1963, as the (280 acre) site for a major man-made fibres plant. For the production of nylon yarn, a labour force of 500 was engaged by British Enkalon, a subsidiary of Algemene Kunstzijde Unie N.V. HQ at Arnhem, Holland. Within a year Enkalon was employing 700 at Antrim and with the expansion into the manufacture of carpet yarns, thousands more job opportunities presented themselves in the next couple of decades.

The three thousand residents of Antrim at the start of the 1960s were served by eighty shops but the absence of local industry meant that Antrim was losing almost 70% of its trade to Ballymena. However, the establishment of British Enkalon, together with the Matthew Report (1963) and Wilson Report (1965), led to draft plans for 'Antrim New Town' – nominated as one of Northern Ireland's three growth areas – being presented to a public meeting in All Saints' Parochial Hall on 8th March, 1965. Enkalon directors counselled that Antrim's future should neither exclusively nor even principally be dependent upon one firm 'however large and progressive that firm may be'.

Local employers then included the Rural District Council, N.I. Hospitals Authority, Aldergrove Airport and the Admiralty, Ministry of Agriculture and Forestry Division, Vauxhall Motors Ltd., garages and service stations, shops and schools.

Castle Street (before redevelopment)
– Courtesy of V. Phelim.

By 1969, the population having increased tenfold, the Railway Street County Primary School (founded 1955), had 525 pupils on the rolls and classes were spilling over into the old Massereene School. 306 pupils attended the Oriel Road Voluntary Primary School. The Lough Road Secondary Intermediate School (founded 1961), catered for 401 pupils, and the thirteen rooms of the Technical School (founded 1931), were used by 210 full-time, 22 part-time day-release, and 461 part-time evening students. But over 300 pupils had to leave Antrim each day to find grammar schooling.

With a population growth to 69,000 anticipated, the prospect of some 14,000 jobs at British Enkalon, 24,000 vehicles passing through the town centre each day of the week, the motorway from Belfast already skirting advance factories in the new industrial and service industry estates to the town's north and east, and Antrim officially accorded the status of Borough, the Seventies realised something of the planners' dreams for administration, education, health, transport, recreation and housing.

Antrim of the 1960s – with its 85 houses in Riverside, 140 at Oriel and Menin roads and 500 between Castle and Fountain streets – mushroomed: extensive housing estates (with community centres) flourished, particularly with the unforseen arrival of thousands of people from more-troubled parts of Ulster.

Aldergrove, on Antrim's doorstep, replaced Nutts Corner as the Province's official airport on September 26, 1963. And Antrim's young people found sophisticated educational facilities in modern nursery and primary schools; 'High', 'Community' and grammar schools at secondary level; and a new College of Further Education. For their teachers, the old Technical College was transformed into a Teachers' Centre and Education Board Resource and Reading Centres.

The old Unitarian manse – 'Castle Puff' – became a home for the *Antrim Guardian* newspaper which chronicles the weekly history of modern Antrim; and future historians will bless Pat McGuigan for capturing on film all that matters, and more! The *Ballymena Observer* also produces an Antrim edition.

Superb recreational and social amenities were made available in 1972 with the opening of the award-winning Antrim Forum: Northern Ireland's first multi-purpose recreation centre; one of the most comprehensive recreational areas in Western Europe. The Antrim Forum quickly proved to be a first-class investment – attracting everyone from Ulster's amateur sports enthusiasts to Olympic gold medalists – with international competitions featuring in live, networked television programmes.

Finally, a silent revolution went on unnoticed in the heart of Antrim between the mid-19th and 20-th centuries: High Street and Fountain Street shrank! Church Street, which excluded the parish church, began at the present Nos. 6 (south side) and 17 (north side). Where Fountain Street today encounters the upper limit of Church Street, the former used to divert through The Well entry to continue for a short distance behind Church Street's (*c.* 1860) 'Black Row' (Nos. 83-75). Today Church Street has a wobble in its middle and Castle Street has all but disappeared.

WORTS AND ALL

A riverside walk (as well as a road) links The Forum with a caravan park and fifty-berth marina at the old 'Corrigan's Cutts' of the Sixmilewater. The European

High Street, Antrim – Courtesy of N.I.T.B.

Community has designated the river a game fishery.

As we stroll along the riverbank, kingfishers 'catching fire' as sunlight flashes on their wings triggers a memory of W. S. Smith's delight in observing the Sixmile's kingfishers back in 1888.

When W. S. examined these exceptionally rich banks, he found Adder's Tongues, Woody Nightshades, small Field Gentians and the hemlock Stork's Bill. In the river itself he found the curious Branched Bur Reed, Flowering Rush and the rare Marsh Nasturtium. Among other rarities were the Field Chickweed, Meadow Rue and Evening Primrose. And there were worts galore: Soapwort, Moon-wort, the blue Milk-wort, Marsh Ragwort and the white daisy-like flowers of the Sneeze-wort Yarrow.

By the time W. S. could hear lake water lapping with low sounds by the shore (accompanied nowadays by the susurration of plaguy chironomids' wings), he had reached a veritable paradise for the botanist. Here, where he found the rare 'Water Hemlock' and equally rare and handsome lily-like floating 'Water Villarsia' or 'Flagrant Agrimony' (the rarest of all), among the multiplicity of wild flowers and rare grasses flourishing today, we may still admire (but never pick) *Spiranthes romanzoffiana:* the extremely rare 'lady's tresses' orchid; originally introduced from America, this lakeshore is thought to be the first place in Europe where it flourished. Attempts to pick this plant (whose creamy-white flowers spiral around the stem), invariably destroy the tuber!

SHANE'S CASTLE

The waters of the Sixmile wending their way into Lough Neagh draw the spectator's eye along the great wooded demesne to the ruins of Shane's Castle.

The descent of the O'Neill of Clanaboy is through both Louis 14 of France and Philip of Spain from Charlemagne (Holy Roman Emperor), and from the ancient Gaelic Iron Age pagan kings of Tara, making them Europe's oldest dynastic family, having been authenticated as far as 360 A.D.!

They were the first Irishmen to have a surname; it derives from 'grandson of Niall' – King Domnall's recognition of his grandfather, King Niall 'Black-Knee'.

The Red Hand of the O'Neills – prominently displayed at the flamboyant Tudor-style gateway to the Shane's Castle demesne – was adopted as the emblem of Ulster.

Shane's Castle Entrance
– Courtesy of Pat McGuigan.

The O'Neill hand is, properly, the right hand, or Dextri Dei (Right Hand of God); first adopted by Hugh O'Neill in the 14th century. Wherever you see the Red Hand of Ulster depicted as the left hand (at the Ulster Hall, Belfast, for example, or on the Massereene shield at the Market Square entrance gate to Antrim Castle Grounds!) you are looking at ignorance; appropriately called a 'sinister' hand, a left, and invariably-bloody hand (giving rise to a yarn about an ancestral warrior-mariner throwing his severed hand ashore to claim Ulster) is a European import from the last century.

The Shane O'Neill who gave his name to the 16th century fortress at the fishing village of Edenduffcarrick was not the celebrated Prince of Ulster but the Clanaboy, Shane McBrian O'Neill. During the late 16th century, the Gaelic Clanaboy and Tyrone O'Neills combined in resistance to the English in Ulster. In 1597 the Lord Deputy learned that Belfast Castle had fallen to Shane: 'all the English men in the ward were hanged and their throats cut, and their bowells cutt oute of their bellyes by Shane McBrian.'

When Shane's eldest son, Sir Henry (who married the daughter of Elizabeth 1's Deputy, Strafford, and inherited the castle in 1616), took his daughter – Rose O'Neill – to Charles 1's Court, the girl was befriended by Princess Mary. When the princess married the Prince of Orange, Rose moved into the Dutch palace as the lady-in-waiting. There she is reputed to have had great influence and to have been nanny to the young William, whose later exploits in Ireland as King William 3 earned him a reputation in Ulster which still survives.

Lady Rose inherited Shane's Castle in 1638 and became Marchioness of Antrim by choosing a husband from among her ancestral enemies – Randal, heir of Sorley Boy, chief of the North Antrim Macdonnells and Marquis of Antrim. Rose was deeply in love with Randal, though she was a staunch Presbyterian and he a committed Roman Catholic.

Rose renamed the local town of Mullynierin ('the iron works', or 'mills') – Randalstown, in honour of her husband. And Charles 2 issued a Charter (1683): 'The town of Ironworks, alias Main-Water, with its rights, members, and appurtenances within the said Manor, should be called for ever by the name of the Borough of Randalstown, and by that name . . . constituted a free borough'. Rose's sweet-smelling message for feuding Irishmen is very clear – 'make love, not war!'

Rose encouraged the settlement of great numbers of Scottish tenants:

> "She seems to have taken great interest in the prosperity of her tenantry and to have exerted herself in their improvement. To her exertions it is said Randalstown was indebted for the manufacturies which were established in it, as also for its being created a borough, and she is said to have encouraged habits of industry and regularity throughout her vast estates."
>
> Drummaul Parish O.S. Memoir

Following her death in 1695 and she being childless, her father's will stipulated that the estate should transfer to his brother, Arthur, but he too was dead. The latter's only surviving heir, Col. Cormac O'Neill, had commanded a regiment for James 2 at the Boyne and the Treaty of Limerick had forced him to flee to France. Cormac

Shane's Castle.

never married so Shane's Castle was offered to his eldest nephew, Henry. Unfortunately, Henry was drowned during his voyage home to Ireland. Next in line was his brother, Ensign Arthur, but a French mob had killed him after he had flung a glass of wine from his Flanders hotel window at a Blessed Sacrament procession passing below. His younger brother, consequently, inherited the property. This was Col. Charles – an ultra-Protestant supporter of the House of Hanover – but he had only ten years in the castle before he died, childless. Once more the inheritance went in search of an heir.

The grandson of Phelim Duff, Sir Henry's second brother, was deemed to be eligible. This was 'French John', 1st Viscount O'Neill, who disinherited his son (Henry), on the pretext that he had married the widow of a tenant. Though French John left the castle and estate to his second son ('Protestant Charley'), Henry's descendants ultimately succeeded and from him are descended the modern O'Neills. 'Protestant Charley' died from over-excitement at Broughshane's old racecourse when his favourite horse won; 'Poddreen Mare', curiously, died that same day: June 7, 1769.

The 1st (and only) Earl O'Neill – the 2nd Viscount, Charles Henry St. John – was a member of the Irish Parliament by the age of 21. (His father was mortally wounded at the Battle of Antrim in 1798.) While he was responsible for the construction of the estate's boundary wall along the Antrim-Randalstown road, his teenage bride made many tasteful improvements in the castle and its grounds.

Shane's Castle had been 'modernised' by 1780, but in 1803 the Earl commissioned Nash – the Prince Regent's famous architect who had designed Buckingham Palace, Regent Street and Regent's Park in London – to redesign Shane's Castle to face south rather than east.

However, Nash's work on the first floor of an extension to the castle was brought to a premature end during a magnificent party at the castle on May 15th, 1816, when a terrific inferno razed the building. *The Newry Commercial Telegraph* reported:

> "The fire, from what we are able to learn, was purely accidental. About eight o'clock, Lord O'Neill and some friends, who were at dinner with him, were alarmed by the report of fire having broken out in one of the chimneys in the northern extremity of the castle. They immediately repaired to the spot, but the passage was so filled with smoke that they were unable to discover the seat of the fire, until the flames were seen bursting through the windows of a room on the third storey. Prompt and strenuous exertions were instantly made to extinguish it, but without effect. The flames rapidly increased and in a few minutes enveloped the whole of that wing, and were presently seen breaking in volumes through the roof. It was then judged expedient to remove the

plate and papers of value; for the effecting of which, his lordship issued instructions with a composure and presence of mind that successfully guided the exertions of his friends and dependants to extricate what was most valuable.

Nothing could exceed the awful sublimity of the scene; the horizon for miles round presented an appearance similar to that witnessed in a summer's morning, before the sun first bursts upon the view; whilst the extensive waters of Lough Neagh displayed a sheet of living flame, reflecting upon the eye of the beholder the steady blaze of the burning pile. The hills and rising ground for miles around were covered by spectators who beheld with profound and stupified astonishment the terrific fire which raged with such violence, that before two o'clock in the morning, a pile of smoking ruins was all that remained of the ancient and magnificent mansion of Shane's Castle, which had braved the storms of so many hundred years."

The family banshee was reported seen hovering above the flames!

Nash's battlemented terrace escaped the fire, as did his conservatory (famous still for its camellias). During the 'Arabian Night's entertainment', which the celebrated 18th century actress Mrs Siddons described attending shortly before the fire, 'the guests plucked their own desert fruit from the exquisite trees of the conservatory, the foot of which was washed by the waves of a superb lake, and the cool and pleasant zephyrs came therefrom to murmur in concert with the harmony from the band of musicians'.

New Shane's Castle – Courtesy of Ulster Museum.

Earl O'Neill salvaged from an English warship, which had sunk in Lough Foyle, the twenty-one magnificent naval cannons which Viscount Baron John Bruce Richard O'Neill made a permanent feature of Nash's terrace; spiked in 1848.

Not until Edward Chichester, Lord Baron O'Neill, took control of the estate was there a building once more worthy of the name 'castle'. He engaged the noted architect, Lanyon, to design the superb Gothic (1865) castle which, unfortunately, only stood at 'the brow of the rock' for fifty-seven years: the castle was burned during the Troubles in 1922.

Arthur – grandson of one-time Vicar Choral of Christ Church Cathedral, Dublin (Rev. William Chichester, 1st Baron O'Neill) – was the first member of the English Parliament to be killed in action during the Great War. Arthur's father survived until 1928 when a grandson, Shane, His Majesty's Lieutenant for County Antrim, succeeded to Shane's Castle. But war came again and Shane was killed (1944), while commanding the North Irish Horse in Italy. His widow, Anne Charteris (a great-neice of Margot Asquith), later married the 'father' of James Bond: novelist Ian Fleming.

Shane's youngest brother – Terence – was the Prime Minister of Northern Ireland from 1963 until his resignation in 1969 at the start of the current 'Troubles'. The son of Shane and Anne – Raymond – is the present (4th) Baron and Lord O'Neill of Shane's Castle, living on the estate in a 1958 Neo-Georgian house. In 1963, Raymond O'Neill married Georgina Montague-Douglas-Scott and to them have been born three sons: Shane, Tyrone and Rory.

So long as 'the black head' carving hangs on the square south tower of the castle ruins, so long will the O'Neill never lack a direct heir, according to tradition. The imminent death of a member of the family, according to another tradition, is heralded by a visitation from Kathleen, the banshee, who, as a child, was stolen by the fairies when her father – an O'Neill lord – once upon a time interfered with a fairy-thorn tree growing by the lough shore.

LOUGH NEAGH CRUISE

All aboard the powerful, twin-diesel *Maid of Antrim* can look forward to a memorable expedition into Ulster's great 'inland sea' and historic east-west divide. Come, cruise with me on a voyage of exploration into the rich inheritance of our past.

Though five of Ulster's six counties border this great liquid sky, about half of the shoreline belongs to Antrim. Being some 17 miles long and 11 miles wide, Lough Neagh is the largest lake in the British Isles; almost the size of Lake Geneva.

Sadly, even on a delightful summer's day cruise, reflections of man's inhumanity to man are inescapable here; a reminder of our area's vital role in the Allies' preparations for the World War 2 invasions of Europe and N. Africa looms before our vessel in the shape of the derelict remains of the freshwater-testing torpedo platform, constructed by the Admiralty in 1942. Reluctantly, one may also recall that fiery Battle of Lough Neagh, fought here in 1642. More reluctantly, one might note that in 1842 the *Countess of Caledon* came to grief just up ahead of us, near Shane's Castle. The *Countess* was the first iron lake-steamer in Ireland. She ran aground with thirty passengers on board, sending her captain head-first into the lough!

All along this shore, a 3 ft guage railway carries restored vintage steam-engines and coaches ferrying passengers from the tiny Antrim station, through the R.S.P.B. Nature Reserve, to the ruins of Shane's Castle, seat of the Clanaboy O'Neills. The rolling-stock includes closed 1930s carriages which originally ran on the Charleoix Tramway in Belgium. As well as the Shane's Castle Railway, the Estate is also the exquisite setting for annual Vintage and Classic car rallies and traction engine rallies. In 1982, Lord O'Neill hosted here an international gathering of the O'Neill clan; the first inaugural ceremony of an O'Neill Chieftain – Jorge O'Neill, a Portuguese noble – to take place for 434 years.

We pass Mainwater Foot – noting that although eight rivers contribute to the lough, only one drains it (the Lower Bann, Ulster's longest river). Once, when the river was blocked by ice, the lough drained south to the sea at Newry!

There's a fine view of Randalstown Forest, with its Elizabethan white deer and red squirrels, on our way to the old 13th century church at Cranfield, where Antrim Borough Council have provided excellent car parking facilities.

On Midsummer Eves, in centuries past, the lough became the world's biggest spa because of its fabled healing powers. Names like Washing Bay, Holy Pool and Holy River testify to the tradition of 'taking the water'; some have claimed that 'Neas' (Irish, signifying an ulcer or sore), is the derivation of the lough's name.

The most ancient (Gaelic) explanation of the name mentions neither any notion of a glacial puddle left behind after the last Ice Age (and trapping the saltwater herring, the pollan, in the lough), nor anything about the gigantic Finn MacCuil tearing out the lough basin in a fit of pique to deposit same, as the much smaller Isle of Man, in the Irish Sea.

To the Boyne, say the old Gaelic annals, fled Ecca, a prince of Munster, when his royal father horsewhipped him and a thousand of his followers from the Province. Angus McIndoe slammed the doors of his Boyne palace in Ecca's face. When Ecca refused to leave, McIndoe slew the Munster-men's horses. With not a little plain horsesense, Ecca observed that he was unable to leave as now he had no means of transport (other than Shank's Pony). Being quite adept at horsetrading, McIndoe acquiesced by saddling Ecca and his people with an enormous magical white horse, but warned that the quadruped must never rest or catastrophe would follow.

Dismissing McIndoe's blarney as whitewash, Ecca's people secured their possessions to the beast's back and resumed their flight northwards, until they reached the Plain of the Grey Copse, in the centre of Ulster. Here they decided to stay and, beneath a spreading horsechestnut tree, unloaded their chattels, quite forgetting McIndoe's injunction to keep the animal on the hoof. Tragically for the old white horse, a spring instantly burst forth beneath him. Not wanting to flog a dead horse, Ecca hastily converted the spring into a well, secured the top with a flap, and instructed a woman to tend the well while he set about constructing his palace and city.

One fateful day, however, the woman's pony-tail became entangled in the flap's hinges and the water burst forth, uncontrollably, overflowing the well and submerging Ecca's palace and his city. That lively chaplain to the Norman King John, Giraldus Cambrensius, calculated that it took but an hour for the spring to transform the Plain of the Grey Copse into the great sparkling lake of Ecca – 'Lough n'Ecca' – Lough Neagh!

Temper your horse-laughs with the corroborating allusion to Ecca's fate in the melodious lines of Thomas Moore's, *Let Erin Remember:*

> On Lough Neagh's banks where the fisherman strays,
> When the clear, cold eve's declining,
> He sees the round towers of other days
> In the waves beneath him shining.

Recently, as we watched the white horses thundering towards Lough Neagh's banks, my children learned from me that Ecca lives on as the 'Horse-God' and 'Lord of the Underworld', and from my wife there sparkled a corroborating wink and a nod.

During the 18th century, Lord Bristol, bishop of Derry, insisted: 'In a monastery on the Continent a manuscript existed, which mentions, that in the 6th century a violent earthquake had thrown up the rock at Toome, which, by obstructing the discharge of the rivers, had formed this body of water, and that L. Erne, in the county of Fermanagh, was produced at the same time'!

With ease, the *Maid of Antrim* rides the white horses as she crosses to the uninhabited, picturesque Ram's Island, anciently called 'Inis Garden'. It is thought that there was a monastery there in the 11th century but that it was destroyed by its pagan parishioners from the Antrim 'mainland' in 1121; perhaps because the monastic house had suffered in the tremendous gale of that year which also destroyed Armagh's round tower? The 42 ft. stump of Ram's Island round tower still stands, obscured from view by the tall beech trees where herons – our biggest wading bird – build enormous nest-platforms. What a delight to watch the herons fishing, as they love to do, in the shallow water. Troops who visited the island during the last war 'invaded' the island's old Swiss-cottage summer residence (and pleasure grounds) of Shane's Castle O'Neills. The O'Neills had their own steamboat on the lough back in the 1830s.

This (east) Antrim shore is famed for the fabulous power of the water to petrify wood which has been submerged for several years. 'That part of the tree that is buried in the mud will become iron, that touched by the water become stone, and that part above the water remain wood', runs Boetius' 12th century report. Petrified holly, resembling pumicestone, made a perfect cutting instrument for sharpening scythes, knives and gentlemen's razors in the last century and encouraged the proliferation of pedlars at Irish fairs, crying:

Lough Neagh hones! Lough Neagh hones!

Put in sticks and brought out stones!

The lough's fishermen never needed the oatmeal-coloured 'hones' if reports are accurate that they simply turned up their trousers and sharpened their razors on petrified shin bones!

It is hard water that petrifies; very hard water indeed! Cruelly, legend must bow to truth, however: many samples of 'petrified' wood have been found over the centuries in rivers more than half a dozen miles east of Lough Neagh and far above lough level; the silica salts which fossilise wood by coagulating in its pores originate in these few small rivers which also deposit such salts and 'petrified' woods near their lough estuaries.

Here too, between the Clady and Crumlin rivers, men of old have known about (and mined) 'brown wood coal'; intermediate between bituminous coal and peat. Two beds, each 25 ft thick, were positively identified as early as 1812; mines operated then between Crumlin and Ballinderry. Test drills at that time also identified at least two other stratum. Northern Strip Mining, at the time of writing, have identified some 70-100 million tons of lignite here and have planned for mining operations at Aghandarragh, Ballyvollen and Ballyshanaghill. This Crumlin Lignite Plan is expected to yield about 1¼ million tons of lignite per year for fifty years.

Our lough adventure continues, rounding Gartree Point where we can catch glimpses of the famous war-time USAAF site – Langford Lodge. Langford Lodge was also the ancestral home of Gen. Sir Edward Pakenham who led the British to defeat at the Battle of New Orleans, 1815. Pakenham was killed at New Orleans by Gen. Andrew 'Old Hickory' Jackson – the son of Carrickfergus emigrants, and one who twice became President of the United States. After World War 2, Langford Lodge had to be demolished, by the RAF. The Pakenhams' pretty Gartree Church, however, remains to delight the eye as well as the soul.

Presently, we cruise past the home of the jolly McGarry bros., captains of the *Maid of Antrim*. Their yard sported elaborate recording facilities during the late Sixties and early Seventies when University College, London, conducted oceanography observations there by means of a cable (still linked to the Eiffel-Tower-like structure which we encounter a few yards from the shore). The readings obtained provided a foundation for modern international experiments concerning wave-produced energy.

The nasty little storms which can suddenly brew up on the lough make it officially one of the world's roughest lakes. Though relatively small, these 'microwaves' have a wall-like face which can be lethal for the amateur boatman (particularly when a calm summer surface tempts him far from the shore). This lough has no specialist rescue service! Local tradition holds that 'the lough claims a victim every year'.

Modern guidebooks warn of whirlwinds which, on sultry summer evenings, produce booming noises called 'waterguns'. However, many local fishermen – who pursue the famous salmon-trout dollaghan or lay their 'long lines' from June to September to hunt some of the lough's millons of eels – laugh to scorn the whirlwind-watergun yarn. In times past, they argue, when blasters began their (evening) work in the many quarries around the lough's shores, their explosives would echo across the waters in calm conditions; 'waterguns'?

Our vessel passes the extractor connected to the pumping station on the shore at Dunore Point. Constructed in the mid-1960s, Dunore currently pumps 30 million gallons of water to Belfast and 5 million to Antrim each day. On a hot summer's day, it is estimated that the lough loses about 160 million gallons through evaporation.

Fortunately, the Dunore equipment has never had to contend with the kind of winters which, between 1740–1895, periodically froze the lough from shore to shore.

STOWING THE NETS, LOUGH NEAGH, NORTHERN IRELAND R 5509

In modern times, vast sections have frozen solid, certainly, but it's only our great-grandfathers who could tell about roasting cattle at mid-lough barbecues or skating parties dancing eightsome-reels on the ice, or buggy rides from county to county! Massive stones, pushed up by the ice, are common finds along these shores.

Out in the middle of the lough the water is just twelve feet in depth; the southern half generally attains a depth of 20-30 ft; our nothern half is a uniform 30-40 ft deep, though, at one point, there is a 'hole' over 100 ft deep.

Because of the shallow, saucer-like basin, the lough abounds in a rich variety of marine life and food. Men have fished these waters since time out of mind. Today you may even meet Riverside's Hannans over by Shane's Castle trawling their draught nets for pollan, as generations have done.

Fish survival depends on the food supply of midges (chironomids), as do the sedge warblers (who make a heck of a noise for their size). When one despairs of science ever discovering a practical method of reducing the unhealthy numbers of midges which plague us – without affecting the marine life – one might recall the more serious menace of flooding in times past . . .

Generously ignoring Ecca, loughshore folk down the ages complained bitterly that the lough was apt to flood to a height of almost eight feet above normal level. In 1738, the Lord Bishop of Down and Connor reported that the church of Ballyscullen and its parish had been 'entirely drowned, and that a fisherman, having twice removed his habitation, was about to do so again, complaining that he knew not where to set it, for the lough followed him'.

The lough level was lowered (and, consequently, the shape altered) in 1846, 1859, 1900 and 1959. The 2 m high steep bank, some 50-100 m from the present shore, marks the original shoreline when the surface was about 3 m higher than today.

As the *Maid* skirts Antrim Bay the skyline is dominated by Carnearny mountain, first planted in 1929 with the emerald shadings of Norway and Sitka Spruce, Japanese Larch and Lodge Pole Pine, and Noble and Grand Silver firs. Here beside us, between the Deerpark and the car park is Rea's Wood, planted in 1961 with Poplar, Japanese Larch, Norway Spruce and natural common Alder.

Keep an eagle-eye open for widgeon, teal, mallard, heron, curlew, snipe, lapwing, sand-pipers, coots, water hens, jays and, of course, the swans; Arctic geese, too, for there's an old saying that 'when the barnacle flies from L. Foyle to L. Neagh it's a sign of a change in the weather'.

We reach the shore safely beside the Massereene golf links; from here, in January 1931, Kay Don practised in his 'Miss England 2' for the world water-speed record, subsequently set at the River Plate, S. America. Here, too, were dumped the dead and dying 'Croppies' of 1798!

With two 115 h.p. diesel engines, the 50 ton *Maid of Antrim* (registered 1963) herself stirs memories: of the L. Neagh Cruising Company's *White Heather* and *Peacehaven* (reg. 1927) vessels, taking thirty tourists each on excursion cruises pioneered by the *Lough Neagh Queen* in the earliest years of our century; of canals and merchant steamboats (operating between 1820–1860), when one could sail from Belfast, or from Carlingford, through Lough Neagh and along the L. Bann to the North Atlantic ocean; and of tragedies such as the Sunday school outing (aboard *The Shamrock* steam tug), when a lady teacher's dress became entangled in the engine machinery and she lost her life.

The provision of lough cruises, together with all the other valuable facilities in Antrim and its borough area, is a display by the modern Antrim Borough Council of the sort of loyalty to its electorate as had the old Rural District Council when the latter acquired for posterity, from Lord Massereene and Ferrard, the Antrim Castle Grounds.

Antrim 1980 – Courtesy of *Sunday News.*

The 20,065 electorate living within the Antrim Borough boundary in 1972 had, by 1984, increased by 6,983. The new Antrim Borough wards and electorate are as follows:

Aldergrove	1,496
Balloo	1,417
Ballycraigy	1,373
Clady	1,373
Cranfield	1,339
Crumlin	1,391
Drumanaway	1,319
Fountain Hill	1,495
Greystone	1,469
Massereene	1,444
Newpark	1,483
Randalstown	1,346
Rathenraw	1,424
Springfarm	1,389
Steeple	1,557
Stiles	1,442
Tardree	1,328
Templepatrick	1,563
Toome	1,400

Despite the curtailment of some of the planners' dreams of the Sixties, the years of terrorist bombings and shootings (from which Antrim – with its happy community relations – has escaped relatively unscathed), and economic recession (shutting down British Enkalon and postponing such projects as the new Area Hospital), the future for Antrim is encouraging.

The Church has played a prominent role in the story of the Antrim area and in the 1980s places of worship are more numerous than ever:

Apostolic	1
Baptist	1
Church of Ireland	11
Congregational	1
Elim Pentecostal	2
Evangelical	3
Faith Mission	1
Gospel Hall	4
Latter-Day Saints	1
Methodist	2
Presbyterian (Subscribing)	15
Presbyterian (Non-Subscribing)	2
Free Presbyterian	2
Roman Catholic	9

Ratepayers paid virtually nothing for the Borough Council's £1 million conversion of the derelict Clotworthy House into Northern Ireland's first Community Arts Centre – indoor and outdoor theatres, cinema, workshops for local craftsmen and artists, exhibition galleries and administrative facilities. No sooner had the Centre opened – on the Antrim Forum's tenth anniversary – than it attracted world-famous entertainers, writers and artists, staged live radio and television programmes, and attracted home-grown contributions for and by citizens aged from 5 to 95!

If the late Lord Massereene's ghost does haunt the Castle Grounds he must be thoroughly delighted that Clotworthy House is more than living up to his dreams for

Antrim Borough Councillors, 1984 – Courtesy of Pat McGuigan.

Front Row (L-R) Cllrs: T. Grant; J. Graham, Deputy Mayor; J. H. Allen, O.B.E., Mayor; J. Blakely; Mrs C. Cunningham and R. Burns.

Middle Row (L-R) Cllrs: S. Dunlop; F. R. H. Marks; T. E. Wallace; M. Donoghue; C. Quinn.

Back Row (L-R) Cllrs: R. Loughran; S. W. Clyde; J. Heffron; R. Thompson.

it. Perhaps the spectacle of modern youth vandalising this beautiful park recalls for some the fact that certain of today's eminent citizens reduced the spiral walk of the park's ornate and historic 'Mound' to a bicycle dirt-track, half a century ago! Sad to say, a white wall has ever been a fool's paper.

Antrim's Mayor, Councillor Jack Allen, O.B.E. – who, since local government reorganisation in 1973, has served eleven consecutive terms and is currently serving his twelfth term of office – on April 30, 1981, officially opened Phase 1 of Antrim Newtown Developments Ltd central shopping complex: the initial 84,000 sq. ft of 'Castle Centre'; a name chosen to reflect the historic ties with Old Antrim. Its bright, airy atmosphere produced by cleverly designed and heated malls with terrazzo floors and suspended ceilings and lined by more than fifty varied and attractive shop-units, quickly gave Antrim a new heart whose loud beat made it at once a mecca for shoppers from Randalstown, Ballymena, Toomebridge, Templepatrick, Ballyclare, etc.

There have been other developments, of course: Wellworth's department store replaced Hall's Hotel; the new RUC regional 'fortress'; the major research and development Science Park facility proposed for Muckamore; the Old Mill complex at Muckamore once again hiving with flourishing and award-winning businesses; the exciting expansion of Aldergrove to the status of an international airport and Freeport; and (upon which the many modern developments depend), new roads to relieve yesteryear's chronic traffic congestion and pollution of the town centre. Antrim enjoys a location which is both picturesque and served by a route network with a high index of connectivity and efficiency, with a labour force exporting quality workmanship right across Europe, emulating the fantastic success of our Neolithic forefathers who traded with precisely the same markets!

With Concorde having blasted into the sky above Antrim, one is reminded that these are the Eighties, and one prays hopefully for the days that may come. The conservation of Riverside, and the retention, restoration and maintenance of the Antrim Castle Grounds, Clotworthy House, All Saints' Parish Church (with its south transept of the 1596 Elizabethan building, and Massereene memorials), and Pogue's Entry, offers an impressive, historic backdrop to the ultra-modern facilities now provided for Antrim's happy mix of old 'residenters' and those from parts of Ulster and parts foreign who have adopted the Borough as home.

For Antrim, 'the years of marking time are over', concludes Mayor Allen; 'now Antrim can march ahead and become what I have always believed it is anyway – the most progressive town in Northern Ireland'.

* * * * *

"Publish the scratches of this pen?
E'en so; 'twere bad enough to waste
Some hours which ne'er can come again
And some good paper . . . but post-haste
To print the lines . . . I fear my brain
Whirls with the world's degenerate taste,
All modern trash being read with zest –
Still, why should I not scribble with the rest?"

Viscount Massereene & Ferrard, 1912.

Courtesy of N.I.T.B.

PLACENAMES

Antrim: (Oentroibh or Entroia – pronounced Entrove) 'the one ridge'.
Ballycraighy: (Baile-creige) 'rocky town'.
Ballyginniff: 'the town or place of sand'.
Ballynageeragh: 'the town of the sheep'.
Birch Hill: district of birches.
Bleerick
Brettens Walls
Bush/Bushfarm
Camlinn: 'the crooked water'.
Carmavy: 'Maeve's carn or cairn'.
Carnearny: 'the carn or cairn of Eire'.
Caulside: (once Cal(l)side).
Carngranny: (Carn Greine) sepulchral pile of Lady Grainne.
Craigy Hall: (Cregach) 'rocky land'.
Creavery: (Craebhaire) 'a branchy or bushy place'.
Crosskennan: (Cros Cenond or Canon Cross) 'battle of Cenond'?
Crumlin: 'the crooked glen'.
Donegore: 'the fort of the goats' (or 'the bloody fort'?)
Dunadry: 'the middle fort' or 'the dun/fort of the oaks'.
Dungonnell: 'Connell's dun or fort'.
Dunsilly: (Dun Sailighe) 'fort of the shallow or common willow tree'.
Farranshane: (once Farinshane).
Gally Hill: (once Gallow(s)hill or Gawley Hill).
Glenmullion: (Gleann Muilinn) 'the glen of the mill'.
Half Umery: (Iomaire) 'a ridge'.
Holy Well: (see 'Steeple Enigma' episode in this book).
Hungry Hall
Hurtletoot: (once Harkletoot).
Irish Town: of English origin?
Islandbawn: of English origin signifying isolated cattle enclosures or farm.
Islandreagh: of English origin signifying the king's inch, or river terrace.
Kilbeg(s): (Coill Bheagh) 'little wood'.
Kilgavanagh
Killead: 'place of many churches'.
Kilmakee: 'church of the son of Hugh (or Mochai,' being Mahee of Nendrum).
Lady Hill
Loughanmore: 'the large pond'.
Lough Neagh: 'the lake of Ecca'.
Maghereagh: (Machaire Riach) 'the grey plain'.
Moilena: (Magh Line) 'the plain of Line'.
Muckamore: (Magh-Comair) 'the plain of the confluence'.
New Park: (once Goosedub).
Niblock
Park Gate: entrance to large park laid out by Sir Arthur Chichester.
Park Hall: (once Porkihaw).
Potters Walls: (?) like Birch Hill, farmed by the Montgomerys of Dervock.
Quarter Lenagh: (Leanach) 'swampy meadow'.
Randalstown: town renamed by Lady Rose O'Neill after Randal MacDonnell, 2nd Earl and 1st Marquis of Antrim.
Rathbeg: 'the little rath'.

Rathenraw: (once Ratlenra).
Rathmore: (Rath Mor Mhuighe Line) 'the great rath'.
Shane's Castle: named after the Clanaboy Shane McBrian O'Neill.
Spring Farme: mid-18th century farm of Lewis Wreyford (or Reford).
Steeple: 17th century Scots settlers' description of Antrim Round Tower.
Stiles: (Stiall) 'a strip of land'.
Templepatrick: 'the stone church of Patrick'.
Tobergill: 'the clear or white well'.
Town Parks
Tullycreenaght: (Tulaigh Cruithneachta) 'wheat hill'.
Whin Park: (Pairc na hAitinne) 'park of the furze or whin'.

Variations in the orthography of a name present many problems of interpretation. The Author invites readers who can provide authoritative interpretations of denominations to communicate with him via Clotworthy House Community Arts Centre, Antrim.

Signed sets of quality prints (each 11¾" × 8¼") from these drawings of Antrim (by Alastair Smyth), to complement *The Story of Antrim,* are available; Tel: Antrim 61984.

Appendix 'B'

SELECT BIBLIOGRAPHY

General History

1. **Antrim & Ballymena Development Commission:** *Antrim New Town Proposals* (1970), pp. 1–20, H.M.S.O.
2. **Antrim Steering Committee:** *Antrim New Town Outline Plan* (1965), pp. 1–52, H.M.S.O.
3. **Armstrong, R.:** *Through The Ages To Newtownabbey* (1979), Shanway.
4. **Bassett, G. H.:** *Book of Antrim; and manual and directory for manufacturers, merchants, traders, etc.* (1888), pp. 13–19, 253–263.
5. **Belfast Directory:** *Business Directory of Belfast,* 1865–6, pp. 235–37, R. W. Wynne, Belfast.
6. **Blair, S. A.:** *Portraits From The Past:* series of articles in *Ballymena and Antrim Guardians,* 1970s–1980s.
7. **Lewis, S.:** *Topographical Dictionary of the U.K.* (1813), p. 37, Lewis & Co., London.
8. **Dublin Penny Journal:** *Antrim Round Tower* (1833), **Vol. 11, No. 55.**
9. **Dubourdieu, J.:** *Statistical Survey of the Parish of Antrim,* 1812.
10. **Griffith, R.:** *General Valuation of Rateable Property in Ireland: Union of Antrim,* 1862, pp. 109–119, Alex Thom, Dublin.
11. **Irish Penny Journal:** *The Town of Antrim* (1840), pp. 89–90, **Vol. 1, No. 12; No. 42.**
12. **Irish Society:** *Historical Narrative, The Hon. Irish Society.*
13. **Laird, J.:** *Ulster Philosophers* (in *Proceedings and Reports of the Belfast Natural History and Philosophical Society*) 1921–22.
14. **Monthly Magazine, the Belfast:** *Sketch of a Ramble to Antrim,* July 10, 1808, **Vol. 2, No. 11,** pp. 421–25, June 1809; **Vol. 3, No. 12,** pp. 5–7, July 1809.
15. **Monthly Magazine, the Belfast:** *Sketch of the Road from Belfast to Antrim,* Oct. 1809, pp. 274–76, **Vol. 3, No. 15.**
16. **N.I. Public Records Office:** *Printed notice from Elizabeth, Countess of Massereene, to the Estate tenants,* 11 March 1805.
17. **N.I. Public Records Office:** *Parliamentary Gazetteer of Ireland,* Pt. 1, 1845, pp. 44–46; A. Fullarton & Co., Dublin, London & Edinburgh.
18. **N.I. Public Records Office:** *Plan of a typical workhouse* (1840).
19. **N.I. Public Records Office:** *The Great Famine in Antrim, Randalstown and districts:* extracts from the minute books of the Board of Guardians of Antrim Poor Law Union 1844–53.
20. **N.I. Public Records Office:** *Ordnance Survey Memoir for the Parish of Antrim,* 1838. (This plus the Memoirs for Drummaul, Donegore, etc., transcribed by B. Trainor, 1969.)
21. **O'Neill, A.:** *Odds and Ends about Shane's Castle.*
22. **Orpen, G.:** *Earldom of Ulster: Inquisitions touching Carrickfergus and Antrim* (in *Royal Soc. of Antiquities of Ireland Journal*), **Vol. 3** (1913) 6th Series, pp. 133–43.
23. **Pilson, J. A.:** *Annals of Co. Antrim* (1847).
24. **Reid, T.:** *Travels in Ireland in the year 1822 exhibiting brief sketches of the moral, physical and political state of the county;* pp. 173–75, (1823), London: Longman, Hurst, Rees, Orme and Brown.
25. **Robbins, J. M.:** *The Lisburn and Antrim Branch (Railway), Rail Mag. 93* (1947) pp. 67–70 illus.
26. **Simmington, R. C. (Ed.)** *The Civil Survey, 1645–46,* pp. 58–60, **Vol. 10** (1961) Miscellancea Dublin: Stationery Office.
27. **Smith, W. S.** *Shane's Castle – a sketch* (1881).

28. **Smith, W. S.** *Historical Gleanings in Antrim and Neighbourhood* 1888, Mayne and Boyd, Belfast; NEELB Area Resource Centre reprint (1979), Antrim.
29. **Stephen, Leslie & Lee, S. (Eds.):** *Dictionary of National Biography,* **Vol. 12,** pp. 163–67, 760–62; London: Smith, Elder & Co. (1908).
30. **Stevenson, J.:** *Antrim,* pp. 33–35; *U.J.A.* **Vol. 10** (1904) 2nd Series.
31. **Young, A.:** *A Tour in Ireland,* 1776–79, **Vol. 1,** pp. 146–52.
32. **Young, R. M.:** *Belfast and the Province of Ulster in the Twentieth Century.*
33. **Young, R. M.:** *Census of Ireland, c.* 1659, S. Pender (Ed.).
34. **Young, R. M.:** *Witchcraft in Antrim,* 1908, *U.J.A. Series 2,* **Vol. 14,** pp. 34–37.

Antiquities
35. **Armstrong, E. C. R.:** 'A bronze bracelet of Hallstatt type, said to have been found near the town of Antrim', *R.S.A.I.J. 6th Series 1* (1911), pp. 58–60 illus.
36. **Bigger, F. C.:** 'Ulster Volunteers of '82: their medals and badges, etc. – Larne, Belfast and Antrim Volunteers'; *U.J.A. 4* (1898), pp. 154–55.
37. **Collis, M. H. F.:** 'Antrim Church Plate', *U.J.A. Series 2,* **Vol. 4,** p. 189 (1898).
38. **Down & Connor Historical Soc. Mag.:** 'Muckamore Abbey'.
39. **Evans, E.:** 'Newly Discovered Souterrains – Co. Antrim'; *U.J.A.* **Vol. 9** (1946) *3rd Series,* pp. 79–83.
40. **Gwynn:** *Medieval Religious Houses: Ireland;* pp. 188–89, Longman, 1970.
41. **Moore, C.:** 'Antiquities near the town of Antrim'; *R. Hist. Arch. Assoc. Ir. J. 4th Series 9* (1889), p. 252, Cromwell's Tree.
42. **Royal Society of Antiquities of Ireland:** 'Drive to Templepatrick and Antrim, visiting Molusk, Carn-Graine, Donegore and Rathmore'. *R.S.A.I.J. Series 5* (1905) pp. 288–93. R. Tower.
43. **Smith, W. S.:** 'Antrim – Its Antiquities and History'; *B.N.F.C., 2nd Series 4* (1894), pp. 13–19.
44. **Vinycomb, J.:** 'The Speaker's Chair and the Mace of the Irish House of Commons', illus. (Antrim Castle); *U.J.A.* **Vol. 10** (1904), pp. 97–100.
45. **Vinycomb, J.:** 'Seals and Armorial insignia of corporate and other towns in Ulster'. *U.J.A. 2nd Series 4* (1898), pp. 23–32 (includes Antrim).

Antrim Castle
46. **Adams, C. L.:** *Castles of Ireland: Antrim Castle* (1904), pp. 9–14.
47. **Deane, C. D.:** 'The legend of ancient Antrim Castle', *Ulster Comm.,* July, 1964, pp. 10–11, illus.
48. **Irish Penny Journal:** 'Antrim Castle, the residence of the Earl of Massereene' (sic) pp. 329–30 **Vol. 1, No. 42** (1841).
49. **Malcolmson, A. P. W.:** 'Election Politics in Borough of Antrim': 1750–1860; *Ir. Hist. Stud.* (1970) **Vol. 17,** pp. 32–57; No. 65, pp. 32–35.
50. **Malcolmson, A. P. W.:** *Extraordinary Career of 2nd Earl of Massereene,* 1743–1805; P.R.O.N.I. (1972) illus.
51. **Marshall, J. J.:** *Lough Neagh in legend and in history* (includes origin of Antrim town, the castle and legend), pp. 64–85.
52. **O'Neill, C. H.:** *Antrim Castle, seat of Rt Hon. Lord Viscount Massereene and Ferrard, Baron of L. Neagh; Dubl. Alex. Thom.* (1860), pp.1–37.

Architecture
53. **Getty, E.:***The Round Towers of Ulster: Antrim* (1856), *1st Series,* pp.131–34, *U.J.A.* **Vol. 4.**
(See also 'Antrim Round Tower' in *Royal Soc. Antiq. Ir. Journal,* 1905, *5th Series,* pp. 292–93; and *'Round Towers of Ireland',* G. Barrow, Academy Press, 1979).

54. **Girvan D.:** List of historic buildings, groups of buildings, areas of archaeological importance in Antrim and Ballymena, Muckamore, Galgorm, Randalstown, Gracehill, Ahoghill, Broughshane, Kells, Connor and Mossley (1969) *Ulst. Arch. Heritage Soc.*

55. **Historic Buildings List:** Historic buildings of special architectural or historic interest, district of Antrim (1974) No. 10.

56. **Irish Builder:** 'Ballycraigy Manor, Antrim'. (Oct. 15, 1869).

57. **Irish Builder:** 'New Masonic Hall, Antrim'. (1881, **No. 23**).

1798 Battle of Antrim

58. **Belfast Newsletter (June 1798):** June 8, 12, 15: Accounts of Battle; June 18: death Lord Vis. O'Neill; 26 Apr. '99: court-martial; 18 June '99: court-martial; 2 & 4 Feb 1800: letters from Antrim; 4 Mar. 1800: Death of Roddy McCorley.

59. **Bigger, F. J.:** *Northern Leaders of '98: No. 1 – William Orr;* Maunsel, Dublin (1906).

60. **Dickson, C.:** *Revolt in the North,* Battles of Antrim and Randalstown, pp. 127–37 (1960); Report of Battle of Antrim by Col. James Durham (Fife Fencibles) to Gen. Nugent, pp. 244–45.

61. **De Barra:** *Ulster in '98,* pp. 7–10.

62. **Fitzhenry, E. C.:** *Henry Joy McCracken;* 164 p. bibliog. *(Ch. 5: The Antrim Campaign,* pp. 108–29); Dublin: Phoenix Pub. Co. (1936).

63. **Hope, J.:** *Memoir of Henry Joy McCracken.*

64. **Keen, J.:** *Memoir of James Keen,* Wesleyan Society Antrim (1798).

65. **Latimer, W. T.:** *Ulster biographies relating principally to the 1978 Rebellion;* 112 p. (Henry Joy McCracken, James Hope, Henry Munro, etc.); Belfast: Jas. Clealand, Wm. Mullan & Son (1897).

66. **Madden, R. R.:** *Antrim and Down in '98:* the lives of Henry Joy McCracken, Jas. Hope, Wm. Putnam McCabe, Rev. Jas. Porter, Henry Munro; 247 p. *(c.* 1920), Glasgow R. & T. Washbourne.

67. **McFerran, J:** *Rebellion of 1798; sketches and incidents of the battles of Randalstown and Antrim,* 32 p. (1898), Belfast: W. & G. Baird.

68. **McSkimmins:** *Annals of Ulster* (1849) includes Antrim 1798.

69. **Musgrave, R.:** *Rebellions in Ireland* (1801).

70. **Observer, Mourne:** *Betsy Gray.*

71. **Observer, Ballymena:** *Walks about Ballymena: a history of the 1798 Rebellion in Mid-Antrim* (1857–58).

72. **Pakenham:** *Ulster Will Fight* – '98 Rebellion in Antrim.

73. **N.I. Public Records Office:** Education facsimile: *United Irishmen,* **Nos. 71, 78;** '98 Rebellion, **Nos. 84, 85.**

74. **Purdon, H. S.:** Battle of Antrim extract from *'Memoirs of Service of 64th Reg., 2nd Staffordshire';* *U.J.A.* 2nd Series 8 (1902), p. 96.

75. **Smith, W. S.:** *Memories of '98* (1895) pp. 8–46.

76. **Young, R. M.:** *Ulster in '98: episodes and anecdotes* (1893), pp. 1–13, 68–72; Belfast: Marcus Ward. Includes: Antrim, Broughshane, Ballycarry, Slemish.

Church history

77. **Collis, M. H. F.:** 'Antrim Parish Church for 300 years'; *U.J.A. 2nd Series 3* (1897), pp. 30–39, illus; pp. 90–98.

78. **Hamilton, T.:** *History of Irish Presbyterian Church* (1887), Edinburgh: T. & T. Clark.

79. **Majury, M.:** *1st Antrim Presby. Ch: over 300 yrs. of Presbyterianism in Antrim,* (1935), 28 p. illus. Belfast: Newton Pub. Co. N.D.

80. **O'Laverty, J.:** *Hist. account of Diocese of Down and Connor,* **Vol. 3** (1884), Dublin: Jas. Duffy & Sons; reprinted 1981, Davidson, Ballynahinch.

81. **Smith, W. S.:** Early register of Old Presby. Congregation in Antrim (1899), pp. 180–90 (Register covering 1674–1736), U.J.A. 2nd Series 5.
82. **Smythe-Wood, P.:** Record of Presbyterians in Co. Antrim (1969), pp. 95–96; *Irish Ancestor 1.*
83. **Ware, Sir J.:** Extracts from Prior Laurentius' 1356 register of Muckamore Abbey (1624) in British Museum; a translation of Ware's Mss. appears in Rev. L. McKeown's *'Abbey of Muckamore'*, pp. 65–66.
84. **West, T.:** Historical sketch of 1st Antrim Pres. Ch. for Coronation Bazaar, June 1902; 26 pp. Belfast: Baird.
85. **Baird, W. J.:** *270 years of Presbyterianism in Killead,* 1625–1895; published in book form by *The Ballymena Observer.*

Literature
86. **Birmingham, G.:** *'The Northern Iron'* (contains dramatic semi-fictional account of Battle of Antrim, 1798).
87. **Irvine, A. F.:** *'My Lady of the Chimney Corner';* Appletree 1980.
88. **Irvine, A. F.:** *'The Souls of Poor Folk';* Appletree 1981.
89. **Irvine, A. F.:** *'Anna's Wishing Chair',* and other short stories (of Old Antrim); edited by Alastair Smyth and republished in 1984 by Appletree as *'The Chimney Corner Revisited'.*
90. **Irvine, A. F.:** *'My Cathedral'.*
91. **Irvine, A. F.:** *'The Man from World's End'.*
92. **Irvine, A. F.:** *'From the Bottom Up'.*
93. **Irvine, A. F.:** *'God and Tommy Atkins'.*
94. **Irvine, A. F.:** *'The Life of Christ'.*
95. **Irvine, A. F.:** *'The Soul of a Slav'.*
96. **McCluney, I.:** *'Autumn Anthology'* (poetry), 1975, pp. 209–12.
97. **Stevenson, J.:** *'Antrim'* (poem) *U.J.A. Series 2* **Vol. 10** (1904).
98. **Heaney, S.:** A Lough Neagh Sequence (poetry) in *'Door Into The Dark'* (1969), London: Faber and Faber.

Maps
99. **H.M.S.O.:** O.S. maps for 1833, 1857, 1902, 1962, 1965.
100. **P.R.O.N.I.:** Antrim (town) 1833, 1859, 1966.

Valuation Records
101. **Griffith:** 1862 general valuation of rateable property in Ireland: Union of Antrim.

Textile Industry
102. **P.R.O.N.I.:** Correspondence, deeds, maps, books, invoices, illus., among collections:
Chaine, William & Son, Muckamore 1874–93;
Black, James & Co., Randalstown 1882;
Coggrey Linen Mill, Doagh 1900–57 (100 vols.);
Doagh Flax Spinning Co. Ltd 1877–1901;
Dunadry Bleaching Co. 1893–94;
Macaulay, P. flax spinner Randalstown *c.* 1857;
Old Bleach Linen Co. Ltd Randalstown 1923–45 (34 vols.);
Roughfort Bleaching & Dyeing Co. Ltd 1880–1900;
and
Ulster Woollen Co. Ltd Crumlin 1906–35 (*c.* 242 vols.)
Ref. details given in P.R.O.N.I. catalogue: *The Ulster Textile Industry* (1978).

103. **Antrim Teachers' Centre:** Old Bleach Linen Company, Randalstown: 35 mm slides with notes on the chain of production. (The Centre has also produced for schools impressive sets of 35 mm colour slides and an 80 page handbook – 'Shane's Castle Farm Study' – with detailed studies of the dairy herd, silage making and the sheep flock.)

104. See also the collections of local branch libraries, N.E.E.L.B. Library HQ, Belfast Central Library, the Linen Hall Library, the Public Record Office and the Ulster-American Folk Park, Omagh.

To seriously pursue, for example, a study of 17th–18th century Antrim, one will find in The Public Record Office of Northern Ireland:–

Maps

(a) Petty's baronial maps (1650s) –
Barony of Massereene Ref: T.2313/1/18
Barony of Antrim   Ref: T.2313/1/15
(b) John MacClanachan's map of Massereene estate (1720) – 3 slides Ref: T.1965/1A/3-5.
(c) Lendrick's map of Co. Antrim (1780) Ref: T.1971
(d) Forts in Lough Neagh area (1602)   Ref: T.1244/17
(e) Baronies, parishes, churches, canals (1807) Ref: T.1129/234
(f) O.S. maps (1831) Ref: O.S.1/1/50

Leases

  (i) 1618 Lease Ref: D.778/1/1
  (ii) 1621 Grant of Antrim Sir Hugh Clotworthy Ref: D. 811/1
 (iii) 1621 Chichester to Sir Hugh Clotworthy: Tuogh of Moylinny Ref: T.956/21
 (iv) 1625 Lease Ref: D.207/14/3
  (v) 1639 Grant of Tithes, Antrim (includes Massereene leases, letters, etc) Ref: D.207/15
 (vi) 1670 Lease: Massereene Fryarye Ref: D.509/24
 (vii) 1696 Lease of manor of Connor Ref: D.1529
(viii) 1699 Lease Ref: D.1905/2/63A/3
 (ix) Massereene Agent's statement of accounts, 1712–14 Ref: D.947
  (x) 19th century leases (often with transcripts of original 17th century lease) Ref: L.P.C. 120–135.

Hearth Money Returns

Consult bound vol. of returns for Co. Antrim (available in Search Room) for lists of people living in and around Antrim during first part of 17th century.

Rent Rolls

1712–13, Antrim. Ref: D.562/834.

Antrim Presbytery Minute Books

1654–91 Ref: D.1759/1A/1–3

Massereene Rental

17th century Ref: T.656/40

Massereene Manuscripts

1605–1713 Ref: T.472

Massereene Rent Ledgers & Accounts

17th century Ref: D.1739

ARMORIAL BEARINGS *(front cover)*

COMPOSITION

The design comprises a complete Achievement of Arms: shield, helm with crest-wreath and mantling, crest, supporters, badge and motto. The shield represents the constitution and character of the area, reflected also in the derivative badge, and the crest and supporters recall the historic families of the area and one of its most important modern activities.

DESCRIPTION

The shield, the basic and most important component, is divided into green and alternate waves of white and blue, symbolising the rural areas and Lough Neagh and Sixmilewater. On the base stands a castle gateway like that leading to the Castle at Antrim, and behind it rises the Round Tower, the famous and historic landmark in the town, which has served as the Council's device. It is flanked by two gold sheaves of barley, an important crop serving the stock-raising industry and suggesting the two rural districts of Antrim and Ballymena. In front of each lies a gold shuttle alluding to the ancient linen-making and more modern textile industries, especially those at Crumlin.

Upon the shield stands the closed helm proper to civic arms, with its crest-wreath and decorative mantling in the basic colours of the shield, green and white. Upon the wreath stands the crest. This is the red eagle with gold beak from the arms of the Pakenham family, which also features in those of the Norman family of De Courcy, connected with the history of the priory at Muckamore. As a symbol of aviation, it alludes, along with the leaves of alder encircling it, to Aldergrove Airport. For necessary distinction it is charged on the breast with gold 'cross moline' of the Viscounts Templetown of Templepatrick.

The supporters represent the two great families of the area, the Massereenes and the O'Neills. The black stags, with gold hooves and antlers, have a ribbon of nylon about their necks alluding to the local importance of British Enkalon and from each hangs a chaplet of gold roses. The stags are a variation of the supporters of the Viscounts Massereene and Ferrard, and are derived from the crest of their ancestors and Clotworthys, so important in the early days of Antrim.

Each stag holds in the mouth the sword from the crest of the O'Neills of Shane's Castle. The motto of the Massereene family, adopted by the former Antrim County Council is very appropriate for the new Borough – 'Per angusta ad augusta': 'Through hard times to prosperity' in the more modern context of the area's development.

The badge is a separate emblem part of the armorial bearings but used on its own for purposes not suitable for the display of the whole Achievement. A major use is that of an Antrim community emblem which can be displayed under appropriate conditions by local organisations, which are not entitled to use the arms of the Council. Necessarily simple, the Antrim badge is derived from the new shield and the former Council's device, showing the gateway, tower and waves from the shield on a green oval edged gold, set on the O'Neills swords crossed diagonally.

INDEX

114

115